Ask the Awakened

Also by Wei Wu Wei

FINGERS POINTING TOWARDS THE MOON

WHY LAZARUS LAUGHED

ALL ELSE IS BONDAGE

OPEN SECRET

THE TENTH MAN

POSTHUMOUS PIECES

UNWORLDLY WISE

Ask the Awakened

The Negative Way

WEI WU WEI

SENTIENT PUBLICATIONS, LLC

First Sentient Publications edition, 2002

Printed in the United States of America

Cover design by Kim Johansen, Black Dog Design
Book design by Ana Dayva

Library of Congress Cataloging-in-Publication Data

Wei, Wu Wei.
    Ask the Awakened the negative way / Wei Wu
Wei.— 1st Sentient Publications ed.
        p. cm.
    Includes index.
    ISBN 0-9710786-4-5
    1. Zen Buddhism—Doctrines. I. Title.
    BQ9268.7 .W45 2002
  294.3'4–dc21

                         2001006859

SENTIENT PUBLICATIONS
A Limited Liability Company
1113 Spruce St.
Boulder, CO 80302
www.sentientpublications.com

DEDICATION AND BENEDICTION

We are all dedicated, though we know it not.

There is only one dedication, for that which we are when we know that we are not is neither subject nor object.

Therefore dedication can only be to the extinction of that which dedicates.

The benediction of those who already know is surely that we may understand the truth that can neither be conceived nor expressed.

This truth is manifest when we know that we neither are nor are not.

In order to see that, we do not have to look, but to cease to look—for, where there is no looking, it is.

When the dreamer wakens
he is absolute absence.

CONTENTS

FOREWORD

My original copy of *Ask the Awakened,* here on the desk beside me, was published in 1963, almost 40 years ago. It is heavily marked with margin notes and underlining, important pages have been turned down at the corners and a bunch of ragged bits of paper are sticking out all over to mark places of special significance. Quite possibly this crisp new book that you are holding in your hands will look just like that in a year or two.

The portrait of Hui Neng, the sixth patriarch, on the frontpiece of that edition instantly reminds me of Wei Wu Wei's deeply penetrating understanding of the early Ch'an masters. I continue to be awestruck by this every time I open one of his books. One can also tell that although he was enormously serious about the subject, it was also a great source of pleasure and fun for him.

There is still no way I can, even now, read the entire book quickly. So, I am writing this introduction also from the perspective of all of Wei Wu Wei's works that I have been fortunate enough to acquire and of my own correspondence with him and his wife, Natasha, and what tidbits others have shared with me who also knew him. I love Wei Wu Wei most of all because he accomplished the impossible with me. He never could have helped anyone else any more than he helped me simply because I had such a long way to come. (He as much as told me so once.) He did so not only with great wisdom, but also with great patience and affection and humor. I owe him a great debt and appreciate him more and more as the wonder of "this" continues to unfold in ever more profound ways, moment by moment.

There are others who know Wei Wu Wei's life history much better than I and there are others who knew the person better than I. I knew Wei Wu Wei only through our correspondence and his books. Soon after discovering one of his books I was lucky enough to have gotten hold of his Monaco address and his real name, for Wei Wu Wei was actually a pen name. It means, as I recall, "action that is non-action," pure function or what he also termed "non-volitional living."

Therefore, I feel the best contribution I could make on the occasion of this very welcome reprint of *Ask the Awakened* is to help new Wei Wu Wei readers with some tips that, from my experience, may be helpful on how to approach this book and find the wonderful treasure that awaits them. For, as I found out when I first urged others to read his books, it is not always immediately obvious that it is a treasure. Somewhat like a mythological elfin city, it may at first look rather unlikely from the outside, but once you have entered you realize you are in a wondrous place.

To begin with, it will help to start this book with the assumption or, if you can manage it, the belief that what Wei Wu Wei is telling us is absolutely true as far as can be expressed. Your own intuition will soon recognize the ring of truth. But it may not be what you expect. And instead of mentally arguing about the parts that one may not agree with or that do not make sense, set that aside for a while and just try to understand how it could be true because he is speaking to us from actual experience, not from conjecture, theory, learned doctrine or even from mere belief. This is a rare opportunity.

Foreword

Wei Wu Wei knew of no fully awakened masters in the West and knew that most of us would never have access to one. That leaves us with only the sutras and writings from the past to work with on our own. Yet often the available translations are flawed because they have been mistranslated by those who have no understanding. However, in the course of his own search he also found a way that we too can awaken on our own. For, in the end, it all comes down to that anyway. It is the "negative way." The negative way can be disconcerting because, instead of learning yet more concepts about what we are, to add to our precious store of esoteric knowledge, as we are accustomed to doing, the negative way is about losing them. Not just losing the "wrong" concepts, but all of them. Since it is impossible to express what-we-are with words or concepts, we may only recognize what-we-are by eliminating what we are not.

Indeed, it can be tough going at first. Wei Wu Wei was a scholar and his facility with languages was considerable. He has used words many of us have never seen before. However, though a scholar, his approach to this matter of awakening is anything but dry and boring. He stalks awakening with great enthusiasm, zest, and wry humor, thoroughly enjoying every minute of the adventure. This is no mere scholarly treatise, but an attack upon your very mind - to cut it off at the root. So, if you are very fortunate and very diligent, this book can take you to a place where you can't advance, you can't retreat and, alas, you have nothing whatsoever left to stand upon. This is his mission.

Yet he does this with such kindness and deftness that we hardly know it is happening until it is too late. He makes it seem like play. He turns the mind's own flawed logic against itself and exposes the illusion that it is. One by one he pries and coaxes from us every precious concept of what we are and every feeble notion of volition. This book is very powerful. He is honest with you. You must be honest with him.

He is precise in his use of words, so that his writing is never sloppy or thoughtlessly crafted as so much of the so-called metaphysical writing is today. If he could find a word that said it better and more concisely he used it. I found I had to keep a large dictionary close by whenever I was reading one of his books. I shared his letters with several other close friends. In one of these letters Wei Wu Wei included the short line, "Life is basically oneiric." Unfortunately none of us knew what "oneiric" meant. We were like the stories told of the seeker who climbs a high mountain in Tibet to reach the great master sitting alone at the summit to ask him the true meaning of life. Here, the answer was in our very hands and we didn't know what the word meant.

A frantic search began. We couldn't find it in any of the dictionaries we owned. (Even now as I write this piece my word processor is underlining "oneiric" in red to tell me it doesn't recognize it. When I clicked on spell check it could find nothing to suggest.)

Even the librarian at the public library didn't know the word and had trouble finding it. Eventually she found a word that sounded like it, but was spelled slightly different. It turned out that Wei Wu Wei had spelled it "differently," but even if he hadn't we would still have had a hard time finding it.

If you don't already know what "oneiric" means I'm certainly not going to spoil it for you by revealing it here. You may look it up as we did and experience for yourself a bit of what we enjoyed. And, yes, it is indeed a good explanation of the meaning of life.

Moreover, I found that his use of unfamiliar (to me) words was actually a great benefit. I didn't realize it at the time, but

Foreword

I had attached habitual, unconscious concepts to the religious, spiritual, philosophical and metaphysical terms I knew. This often blinded me to seeing it any other way. I had overlaid these terms with layers of meanings that turned me in the wrong direction and left no room for new interpretations. With Wei Wu Wei's unfamiliar words, I now had only the barest meaning to go on and, I believe this allowed me to be more open to perceive in new directions.

Some may be put off if they cannot immediately understand a seemingly enigmatic paragraph. But, to be sure, Wei Wu Wei is not just trying to be abstruse. Nor is he being "affected" nor trying to be cute nor deliberately trying to make it harder for us. Actually he is attempting to take us, even prod us, beyond our logic to something that cannot be thought or said. As he told me, "rationality can take you only so far."

It might be assumed that possibly the reason this great "secret" can't be told in words or concepts is just because it is too complicated and esoteric to be explained or that maybe it is so magnificent that the words just haven't been invented yet. Some new readers might even think, "Maybe this fellow knows something I don't. But if he does why doesn't he just come right out and say it?" But Wei Wu Wei demonstrates that it is not that at all, rather it is the very nature of the way the thought mechanism itself works that obscures this most important recognition.

I like paradoxes, those seeming contradictions that bring one's thoughts up short. So personally, I found Wei Wu Wei's distinctive style very enjoyable. For instance, one of my favorite paradoxes is one that came about when a London newspaper publisher was asked, during a newspaper workers strike, what his headline would have been today. He answered, "All is Quiet on Fleet Street."

Foreword

Because I liked paradoxes I do think it helped me to "hang in there" when I was really stumped. A couple of examples of Wei Wu Wei's paradoxes are: "I am, but there is no me." And: "Why are you unhappy? Because 99.9 per cent of every thing you think, and everything you do is for yourself-and there isn't one."

Read this book straight through? Don't even think about it. Not if you are serious about understanding it. Though, if you are not serious, you will never make it through to the last page anyway. I seem to remember that a Wei Wu Wei reviewer said something to the effect that most of the time the book will be sitting, unread, on your knee, while you ponder each paragraph. How often have you encountered a book so filled with meaning that it was able to capture you as completely as that?

Though he has found great meaning in the Eastern religions and holds them in the highest regard he is not over-involved in the affectations and traditions that many in the West seem to think is a necessary part of them. Because Wei Wu Wei has such a profound understanding of Eastern (as well as Western) mystical writings he has been able to go to the heart of them and present their essence to us with a new purity that we in the West can greatly benefit from. This is entirely in the spirit of the original Ch'an masters.

He was, along with Douglas Harding, Robert Linssen, Paul Reps and a few others, (even, in my opinion, Nisargadatta Maharaj) a trailblazer when it comes to creating a wholly Western approach to this ancient insight unencumbered with unnecessary cultural artifices. Although he himself characterized his writings as "an intermediate stage...a presentation in modern idiom supported by the authority of the great masters."

Foreword

His terse statements like, "Cease identification with all phenomenality," are at first puzzling, even frustrating. But then, if it finds any suitable soil to take root it has the power to eventually reclaim the whole mind. I see this seemingly innocuous phrase as working almost like the modern day computer virus. Once it gets into the mind it begins to erase, bit by bit, all that you think you are and all that you think you do and all that you think you have, until the obvious dawns and what-you-are shines forth, breaking through the clearing mists of obnubilation.

Once recognized, there can no longer be any doubt.

GALEN SHARP
August, 2001

INTRODUCTION

Perhaps anyone sufficiently qualified can sit down and write a book dealing with any aspect of human knowledge and maintain that it states categorically the truth in so far as it is known at the time at which he writes. That can be done where objective understanding is concerned. But here objective understanding is not the aim in view, for objective understanding is a dead-end and leads nowhere. That is the reason why the great Masters never methodically taught it. That is the reason why they invariably sought to maneuver their disciples into turning round in the right direction, so that they might one day apprehend the truth for themselves, and subjectively. That truth is always present, and is always exactly where we are.

Occasionally, however, particularly when they were questioned by high officials of the state, they offered objective knowledge, and that is of incalculable value to us, for we have no living Masters at hand to maneuver us into turning round in the right direction, so that we have no alternative but to find out how to do that ourselves; and that can only be done when we have acquired a high degree of dualistic understanding. Such understanding, however, is not an end, but a beginning only, or, if you like, it is the terminus from which the train sets forth that leads directly to our destination, for, henceforth, we may be said to run on rails, in the sense that the road home from objectivity to subjectivity is straight and direct, if it can be followed. This is the "chemin" of which

Shen Hui speaks so often, the "way" which, once "obtained," leads directly to the goal.

Therefore in this little book we continue the journey during which the truth that can never be written is gradually approached by intuition rendered dualistically. As one closes in on that truth that which has been described vaguely is subsequently described more accurately and more fully, and that which was imperfectly comprehended is corrected by that which has later been understood. Only the awakened can say definitely whatever it may be possible to say without error.

The methods of the Masters are illustrated by the saying: "To acquire understanding at the hands of others is to close the gates of self-enlightenment." Nothing could be more clearly or tersely expressed, and the explanation, of course, is that the understanding thus acquired is necessarily objective understanding. In fact my understanding is valueless to you, quite necessarily so, even it be the correct understanding. Perhaps that is not clear, but it is a fact. In objective science my understanding, if it were correct, would be perfectly valid for you and you could take it from me if it were adequately expressed. But this understanding is not of that kind, and it cannot be transferred or transmitted. It can only be pointed at, and you have to find your own way to it yourself. Phenomenally, dualistically, you can be led to within "sight" of it, but only yourself can "see" it. Even that is metaphorical, for the truth can never be "seen," for seeing is objective. That too is looking in the wrong direction, and even when you look in the right direction you will see nothing, that is void, for looking itself is objective and must be abandoned.

Discouraging? Not really. After all, if it were easy should we not all be Buddhas?

I have expressed my view that since we have no fully-awakened Masters available to maneuver us into the correct orientation, we must proceed via objective understanding. Alas, we have no living Masters available in the West at present, as far as I am aware, but we have the great awakened Masters of the past whose words have been preserved, and we have the sutras, in particular the supreme Prajnaparamita sutras. Alas, they are not easy; alas, the translations—for which, nevertheless we should be humbly grateful—are not quite satisfactory; and alas, we do not study them as we might. My view, for anything that it may be worth, is that to all intents and purposes we have nothing else that matters. It is our misfortune that Chinese pictograms are devoid of grammar and syntax, that most words have many meanings, and that only someone who has fully understood the meaning of the text could really be qualified to translate it. Beyond that, many Masters spoke in local dialect, their very method tended towards slang or "argot" the sense of which can only be guessed, and they no doubt used many common words in a special technical sense that is difficult to recover. All that is our burden, and we must bear it as best we may.

We are not helped by our own regrettable tendencies to misuse our own words. Take, for instance "meditation." Exactly what the more qualified people who use it mean by it I do not know, but we all know what the normal man means by it. St. John of the Cross, an Enlightened Christian whose understanding is in perfect conformity with that of the oriental Masters, defines it clearly: he says, "meditation, which is discursive mental activity by means of images, forms and figures that are produced imaginatively," and he goes on to say that it is the first thing to be got rid of. The great Masters said exactly the same, in fact that may be said to be the focalpoint of their teaching, and, even if they had not said it, anyone who understands what they require of us must rapidly see it for himself. Yet, presumably because it is one of the meanings found in a Sanskrit dictionary for the word Dhyana, we are faced with practically nothing but that "method" of "attaining" enlightenment. Of course anyone can take any word and declare that he uses it to mean the opposite, but really that does not seem to be a very good idea, nor one that is calculated to help the struggling pilgrim. The real meaning of Dhyana is well-enough known, though no single word covers it in our languages; of these "awareness" is the nearest, implying a vivid state of consciousness free of all "abiding" or mentation of any kind.[1]

Alas, there are many other such words, not least the unfortunate "Zen." One may have the highest possible regard for the Japanese development of Ch'an, but Zen is that, and nothing else whatever. Moreover Ch'an is not dead, did not die when the doctrine was carried over to Japan; that piece if propaganda is no longer tenable now that we know of the great Ch'an Masters, including Han Shan who restored the monasteries, down to the grand old Master—Ancestor, as they call him—Hsu Yun who died last year at the age of 119. They preserved in far greater purity the teaching and methods of the T'ang Masters, and when we turn to them we find in them a revelation, and it is surely as inaccurate as it is absurd to apply to them and their teaching the Japanese term "Zen" which represents a tradition considerably different. Whatever propaganda and commerce may wish, serious students and scholars should use words in their proper sense.

[1] The Lama Anagarika Govinda defines it variously as "intuitive vision," "inner awareness," "spiritual awareness." Without in any way comparing a definition with his, the sense in which I use it in this book is just non-objective awareness. As substitutes for "meditation"—"contemplation" and "concentration" are equally unhappy: anyone who understands will immediately see why this must be so.

Introduction

As for terms such as "self-nature" that has rarely, if ever, anything to do with what we think of as "self," for it indicates nothing personal, but subjective mind in the non-dual sense of subjectivity; the words "mind," "One Mind," "No-Mind," etc. rarely have the objective meaning we normally give them, and just as wu nien does not just mean "no thought," wu wei does not imply "inaction" but, rather, "spontaneity," so "chih" does not usually mean "knowledge," and "prajna" does not always or even perhaps often mean what we think of as "wisdom."

If this is borne in mind the true sense of the words of the Awakened Masters will rapidly become clearer, and if we re-read them every six months or so we will reap an even richer harvest of understanding, until, finally, we too will have fully and perfectly understood.

PART I

The Cross-Roads

❧

Why are you unhappy?
Because 99.9 per cent
Of everything you think,
And of everything you do,
Is for yourself—
And there isn't one.

1 ~ The Harlequinade

Perhaps our most serious handicap is that we start on the wrong foot. In the end this is likely to be fatal, and, I fear, generally is. We have a basic conditioning, probably in some form of Christian religion, of which little remains today but its ethical content, or in one of the modern psychologies, that of Freud, Adler, or Jung, or in some scientific discipline, all of which are fundamentally and implacably dualist. Then the urge manifests, and we start reading.

Every time we happen on a statement or sentiment that fits in with our conditioned notions we adopt it, perhaps with enthusiasm, at the same time ignoring, as though they did not exist, the statements or sentiments which either we did not like or did not understand. And every time we re-read the Masters or the sutras we seize upon further chosen morsels, as our own jig-saw puzzle builds up within us, until we have a personal patchwork that corresponds with nothing on Earth that could matter in the least. Not in a thousand million kalpas could such a process produce the essential understanding that the urge is obliging us to seek.

We are required to do exactly the opposite of all that. We are required to "lay down" absolutely everything that is "ours," and which is known as "ignorance"—even though we regard it as knowledge. It is like stripping off clothes that have become personal. Then naked, but in a nakedness that does not recognize itself as such, we should go to the Masters, who will clothe us in the garments of the knowledge or understanding that we really need. It is their jig-saw we must complete, not "ours," for their "doctrine," what they have to reveal to us, is one whole and indivisible, and the statements and sentiments that we do not at once understand, rather than

8

those that we think we do, are the ones that matter. One by one as we re-read, and finally all at once, their meaning will become manifest, and we shall at last understand what the Masters have to tell us. Then, and only then, can we acquire their understanding, which is the fulfillment of the urge.

As busy little bees, gathering honey here and there, and adding it to their stock in their hive, we are wasting our time, and worse, for we are building up that very *persona* whose illusory existence stands between our phenomenal selves and the truth of what we are, and which is what the urge in us is seeking. That "laying down" of everything that is "ours" has always been insisted upon by the Masters, but we affect to ignore it, precisely because that very notion of "self" which is the center of what we have to "lay down" seeks to take charge of the operation, and generally succeeds in doing so, thereby frustrating from the start any hope of fulfilling the urge. Is there any wonder that we so rarely get anywhere at all?

It is interesting to note that in the recently discovered collection of sayings of Jesus there is one in which he formally adjured His disciples to divest themselves of all their "garments." It is understandable that such a statement should have been omitted by those later compilers who had no idea what such a requirement could mean. But to us it should be a commonplace. As far back as Chuang-tse we find the story of the old monk who, in despair of knowing enlightenment before he died, went to see Lao-tse. On arrival Lao-tse came out to meet him, welcomed him, but told him to leave his followers and his baggage outside the gate, for otherwise he would not be admitted. The old man had no followers, and no baggage, but he understood, went in and found his fulfillment.

2 · Ask The Awakened

Since Bodhidharma, the recurrent menace that has overshadowed the Supreme Vehicle has been man's infatuation with himself. Whenever the succession of great Masters weakened in power or in quality the self-flattering mirror-polishing doctrine re-emerged.

Hui Neng and Shen Hui rescued the doctrine, but today it needs saving again, for, in the West at least, we are nearly all busy polishing our mirrors, or perfecting the hansom-cab as I have termed it, instead of understanding that neither the polisher nor mirror, perfector nor cab, has ever or could ever exist.

What we need is another Bodhidharma, firm as a rock, fierce as a tiger, merciless in his "grandmotherly kindness," and not afraid to tell Emperors of China that they are talking through their hats. And if we cannot hope for a Bodhidharma, then at least we need desperately a Hui Neng. Otherwise, though Buddhism may survive, the Supreme Vehicle will surely be lost.[1]

And only the Supreme Vehicle ultimately matters, for self-exalting Buddhism is pseudo-Buddhism, for it is a contradiction in terms, a soothing syrup or a drug: only the Supreme Vehicle carries the full and final message of the Tathagata.

As long as we do not perceive the fatuity of a phenomenon telling itself how marvelous it is, we will never come to the knowledge of that which we are when we have understood that, as phenomena, we are not.

---

[1] Hubert Benoit describes Bodhidharma as "an 'Awakener,' someone who comes, with kindness but also with implacable firmness, to rouse us from the dream in which we are living."

3 – The Cross-Roads of Time and Space

"The present has no extension but intensity." (Lama Anagarika Govinda.)

The present has no duration. Therefore it does not exist in the lineal dimension of time. It is not "horizontal." It has only a *point of contact* with seriality.

The extension of the present is in another dimension to that of time. It is therefore at right-angles to time. The direction of measurement of this essentially timeless dimension is—*within*.

That is the reason of the importance instinctively given to *momentanéité*, to "presence in the present," to "spontaneity," and the reason of the creation of expressions such as "the Eternal Present."

The so-called present is our link with the dimension that includes the three we already know and use. It is the point at which Time cuts across Space, and as a concept it is spatial rather than temporal.

The present is not a fleeting moment: it is the only eternity. In Time "lies" *samsara:* in the Present "lies" *nirvana.* Time is the measurement of objectivity: the Present is the presence of subjectivity, in which everything potentially is, and from which, in Time, everything is apparently projected.

The assumed (so-called) present is our point of contact with *bodhi*-mind. It is the invisible portal through which intuition reaches us from the interior of ourselves, from that universal and limitless interior (spatially thought-of) which is all we ever were or ever will be, and which is out of time. It is the sole line of communication between our enveloping totality and our apparent existence as separate individual creatures, between our universality and our illusory

11

particularity, between the noumenality and the phenomenality of all sentient beings.

The present alone in our experience is what IS, and phenomenally it is not; for it is only an imaginary division between past and future—like the equator between the northern and southern hemispheres. It is like a fictional line of latitude that is a symbol rather than an existence, and yet represents a vital transmission from one sphere to another, from north to south, from past to future, neither of which has any reality in itself but each of which is a concept that artificially divides a continuity in space or in time.

The present alone represents that which we are in an apparent world in which we are not, since therein we are appearances (phenomena) only. We ourselves neither exist nor do we not exist. Neither existing *samsarically* nor not-existing *nirvanically,* we are nothing—in any way in which we can know ourselves—but as *the Present.*

Note: The present is the dimension I have indicated by the image of "vertical" being or seeing, which is an essential discrimination for comprehending in what manner we (sentient beings) can be understood to BE. It is also the dimension in which occurs whatever actuality there may be in the expression "living in Zen," and in "when I am hungry, I eat; when I am weary, I sleep"—in the manner in which the awakened Masters themselves did that.

4 ∿ He Who Gets Slapped

When I was a child I was taken to the circus. There I saw a long series of entrancing performances that caused men and animals to execute every kind of astonishing and unexpected maneuver. And throughout, but particularly when the scenario and its appurtenances were being changed, there appeared a grotesque personage, vaguely resembling a human being, who interfered with everything but effected nothing. He fell over the carpets, bumped himself against every object, was slapped and kicked, and then took all the applause as though he were responsible for everything. We thought him very funny and laughed at him like anything.

Now that I am no longer a child he seems to me to be a perfect image of the I-concept, whose function is apparently his, and whose performance corresponds in all respects with that of the clown, in the circus which is our life. In all respects but one: we laughed at the clown in the circus, but we take seriously the clown in the circus of life, although the one is as ineffectual as the other. We even believe that he is responsible for the performance, whereas as children we could see that he was responsible for nothing that happened, that his "will" was totally ignored by the circumstances to which he was subjected, and that in every event he was an unnecessary nuisance.

In one respect, however, our attitude is unchanged: in both the circuses we love the clown dearly and consider him more important than anything else in the show.

5 – That I Am

When I have looked at a jug I have supposed that eye-subject was looking at jug-object. But eye-subject is itself an object, and one object cannot be the subject of another object. Both eye-supposed-subject and the jug are objects of I-subject. That is apparent transcendence of subject-object.

But only when we realize that, in split-mind, I-as-subject must always be itself an object while it also has its own supposed-object, do we understand that this constitutes an infinite regression, and that final transcendence is the understanding that I am not-subject, for, since in reality there are no objects, there cannot be a subject.

No-objects and no-subject constitute impersonality, the resultant of the negation of each member of every pair of opposites, or No-Entity.

Only whole mind can know this, and that is "that I am."

6 ·- Enlightenment by Non-Action

All so-called volition is a manifestation of the I-concept. *Who* seeks enlightenment? As long as it is sought under the compulsion of the I-concept how could it possibly be realized?

On the other hand, as soon as the I-concept disappears, it is seen to be there all the time.

But the I-concept only wants pseudo-enlightenment, by which it can pose as a sage; realization, involving its own liquidation, does not appear at all desirable, and it will place every possible obstacle in the way.

This is the reason why any and every "method," "discipline," etc., subject to the I-concept, must be a path leading away from home. Since all action that is not non-action, or, as we see it, spontaneous, is performed under the compulsion of the I-concept—for there is no other "actor," that is no real "actor" at all—enlightenment or satori can only be the consequence of non-action.

Service

Gratifying the I-concept can never render a service. That, no doubt, is why the Masters never did it, for rendering service was their sole use of living.

Yet it is the sole method of what we regard as rendering service.

7 ·~ Silence, 1

When the Maharshi tells us that silence is a more potent medium than speech we tend to be incredulous, for to us silence is merely the negation of noise.

When he states that "stillness is the sole requisite for the realization of the Self as God," we know that he refers to stillness of the mind. So silence also means silence from thoughts, or, as we might prefer to say, absence of cerebration. The negation of noise as an aid to thought could never be in question, for thought must be a barrier to spiritual understanding.

The potency of silence, of which he sometimes speaks, as indeed do others, is to be sought in the interval between thoughts, of infinitesimal duration to split-mind, but without, or of infinite, duration, in itself, since it is intemporal. To him who experiences it, it might have any conceivable duration, though to an observer it can have none. In itself it is never a momentary thing, for it is the permanent background of what we experience as time, the reality rather than the background, and in a feeble image, the screen on to which the ever-moving pictures of conceptual life are projected.

Its incalculable potency then becomes apparent, for it is no other than whole-mind.

8 ⋅ Reflections

Awareness is I-subject.

Truth is that which lies in a dimension beyond the reach of thought.

What is your trouble? Mistaken identity.

"Birth" is the birth of the I-concept. "Death" is the death of the I-concept. There is no other birth. There is no other death.

The "world" is only a picture projected on to a screen.

I am pure Subject: everything I perceive is my object, but, as object, ultimately my Self.

There is no Path! Paths lead from here to there. How can a path lead from here to here? It could only lead *away* from home.

All *methods* require a *doer*. The only "doer" is the I-concept.

All objects are necessarily untouchable.

Within and without, above and below—what is the resolution of these opposites? A further direction of measurement.

Whole-mind has no "thoughts," thoughts *are* split mind.

The "aggregate of latent tendencies," held together by an I-concept, is that which reincarnates—whatever that may be.

How do we know that the world is transitory, that time is passing, that nothing stands still? We could not know that our river was flowing unless we could put one foot on the bank!

There is no entity, only a continuum—and that continuum is consciousness.

Humility is the inevitable condition resulting from the absence of an I-concept. Without such absence humility can only be a mask for pride, which is its counterpart.

Science is concerned with objects, which are unreal. If it concerned itself with the subject of the objects it might find out what they really are.

Mind is the dynamic aspect of matter.

The "present" does not exist objectively: it is subject itself. The "future" being unknown to us always, we live entirely in the past.

Searching is trying to see the Self (Reality) as an object. But, all the time, that object is Subject.

Karma and Reincarnation, and all and all, belong to the dream-world. The dream goes on....

Meditation is exercising the I-concept.

"He who is in the habit of looking down upon others has not got rid of the *erroneous idea of a self.*" (Hui Neng, p. 40.)

"Non-Action" is what we call Spontaneity.

9 · · *The Readjustment*

Awakening is a readjustment. The state is always present, is our normal, permanent, real nature—as the Masters of all the doctrines never tire of telling us—but the conscious experience of it is denied us by a deviation of subjectivity on to a concept that, as such, is unreal, an object in consciousness appearing as its own subject. Until this phantom is exorcised by being exposed, subjectivity appears to be bound, and we cannot experience it as it is in reality.

When this anomalous situation is understood, we need to start putting this understanding into practice, that is not just thinking about it, but experiencing it. There have been people, apparently born "ready," for whom the fact of understanding has been sufficient in itself to produce the experience, but for the rest of us habit and practice are a necessary prelude to conscious experience of our reality.

However it is important to understand that there is nothing to acquire, but only an error to be exposed, because acquiring necessarily involves using, and so strengthening that spurious "I" whose dissolution we require.

For this merely a readjustment is needed, such readjustment being the abandonment of identification with an inexistent individual self, an abandonment which leaves us unblindfold and awake in our eternal nature.

To seek to persuade ourselves that we do not exist as individual entities is, however, to ask an eye to believe that what it is looking at is not there. But it is not we alone who have no existence as entities: there are not any anywhere in the reality of the cosmos, never have been, and never could be. Only whole-mind can reveal this knowledge as direct cognition which, once realised, is obvious. That is the total readjustment. And only "I" remains.

10 ·– Silence, 2

Silence, regarded metaphysically, is considerably different from conventional silence, dualistically defined, silence as one element in a comparison of opposites, silence as the opposite and complement of noise. The silence which the Maharshi states is more powerful than speech, a more potent medium of instruction than words, the silence in which, and by which, occurs the transmission of mind via mind in which the ultimate doctrine of the Buddha was handed down from patriarch to patriarch according to the Ch'an Masters, is rather the background of the time-illusion, the interval between thoughts that is normally imperceptible to divided mind, of infinitesimal duration, but which is in itself intemporal, of no, or of infinite duration. If we can seize it, so we are told, and hold it, the mind stays open, and we are awake at last.

What, then, is it—this metaphysical silence? Clearly it is the "Buddha-mind" of Ch'an, the "Witness" of Vedanta, the "Father" of Christianity, i.e. whole-mind. The mechanism of dualism seems to be that of the escapement of a clock, which is also an instrument for recording time. One half momentarily stops the flow of time, and then the other, tic-toc, tic-toc. So does each half of split-mind, tic-toc, tic-toc, and the interval between each tick is pure movement, the background, the intemporal reality which, measured by each alternative tick, becomes time as we know it. And the tic-toc, the alternative stoppage, is the comparison of opposites, the activity of split-mind, which we know as thought and mentation.

We can now see why every one of the awakened tells us *ad nauseam* that all we need to do is to arrest the movement of thought in order to know whole-mind and find ourselves awake. It explains also why *wu* or *satori* is always precipitated by a sudden sound, anything from a clap of thunder to the snapping of a twig, or, indeed, any other sensory perception whatever. Such perception momentarily arrests the eternal tic-toc of thought and, the subject being ripe, whole-mind takes possession and is no longer split.

That the awakened continue to know divided mind, in communicating with those who remain identified, is evident, but for them that condition is the abnormal, and the state of whole-mind the normal, instead of the contrary as with the rest of us. But it is surely an error to suppose that we do not know whole-mind in our daily life—for the consciousness that is aware of our having thought is certainly that, a consciousness that is ever awake, is always present, and that alone is "real."

11 ·~ *The Universal Presence*

Subject and object are the essential tic-toc. Phenomena are whole-mind tic-tocking as subject/object, seer and seen, which are a split unity in time.

Every object is a facet of subject, and nothing but subject itself, whereas subject is an objectivisation of subjectivity, and, as such, quite unreal.

Realised, that which is whole and real is mind, unself, the void—or whatever label you may use.

In conceptual language can one point more nearly in the right direction—towards the universal presence?

Note: Split-mind is a time-piece, and, as such its mechanism is an escapement, each half of which momentarily arrests the flow of movement, in alternation—tic-toc, tic-toc.

12 ·~ *Verity*

ONE: What are you and how do you know it?
TWO: I am pure consciousness, and I know it because I love.
ONE: The first is so, the second is not.
TWO: Why is that?
ONE: Because you say it.
TWO: I don't understand.
ONE: Pure consciousness cannot say "I love."
TWO: Why not?

The Cross-Roads

ONE: It cannot be said by pure consciousness, but only by an identified object.

TWO: What then can I say as pure consciousness?

ONE: Pure consciousness cannot say "I love" even via an identified object, but it can say "I am love." If the answer to my question had come direct from wholemind that is the way you would have transmitted it.

TWO: Then those teachers who use the form "I...," in order to reveal the truth, are wrong to do so?

ONE: It might be better to say that the form of words in question is open to objection.

TWO: Because?

ONE: They are speaking to the identified, and the identified cannot speak direct from pure consciousness. Therefore when they repeat the words, applying them to themselves, inevitably the I-concept intervenes and seeks to apply the statement to itself. It cannot be excluded as long as it is there.

TWO: By saying what I am, rather than what I do, that is avoided?

ONE: It is nearer the truth.

TWO: An example to make it clearer?

ONE: As many as you wish: the Maharshi did not love— never, never: he *was* love, or, more exactly, *karuna*-caritas/*prajna*-gnosis. Pure consciousness is and does not.

TWO: And that applies to Jesus also?

ONE: Did he say "God loves" or "God is love"?

TWO: If I have understood, then love itself does not exist, nor hate?

ONE: Of course not.

TWO: Nor impersonal, unpossessive love, asking no return and unaccompanied by jealousy?

21

ONE: That, too, would be a "thing."

TWO: Nor affectivity, knowledge, ignorance, cognition, *prajna, karma?*

ONE: Things, all things! The unending dualistic process of imagining entities and things!

TWO: You have been leading me astray.

ONE: Neither more nor less than those who knew so much better than I. Truth can only be pointed at—*tant bien que mal.* The sages often enunciated an apparent doctrine—and then casually mentioned that of course nothing of the kind really existed. At all costs they sought to avoid the danger of dogma.

TWO: The closer to the truth the less meaning words have to the many?

ONE: At first the words "I am love" would seem nonsense: at the last they alone mean anything.

TWO: Because they alone are nearly true? Or "I am knowledge"?

ONE: Knowledge, cognition, gnosis; love, affectivity, compassion; *prajna, karuna; sat, chit, ananda,* being, consciousness, bliss—none exists as a "thing," and all are one.

TWO: Then "I am consciousness" or "I am being" are better still?

ONE: There is no "better," each is an aspect of the others. But "conscious" needs no "ness," just as "being" can have no article, which would make it an entity, as "ness" would make the former a thing.

TWO: One should be content with "I am"?

ONE: One should hold one's tongue! If you must gab— speak to someone who will understand however incorrectly you say it.

TWO: Then how can one teach?

ONE: Those who were qualified to teach, those few, like the Maharshi, said that silence was more efficacious, but in early stages teaching can only be given via a series of untruths diminishing in inveracity in ratio to the pupil's apprehension of the falsity of what he is being taught.

TWO: That is devastating!

ONE: Not at all: it is just education. Truth cannot be communicated: it can only be laid bare.

13 ⁓ The Kingdom of Heaven on Earth

Philosophers, theologians, moralists, sociologists—anyone who spends time considering the troubles of mankind, their wrongs, griefs, miseries, conflicts, ambitions, personal and general—have analysed these things and attributed them to almost everything from Satan to Heredity. Literature is largely composed of the problems arising from this search for the cause of what is called "Evil."

But you have only to sit back and think for a few moments in order to perceive that what is called "Evil" has only one cause, a most obvious one, that is neither Satan nor Heredity nor anything in between. It is the I-concept, the notion of an individuality, of a separate self.

Take that away, and nothing deriving from it can remain—for all derive from pride, greed, envy, desire, ambition, etc., all of which are manifestations of egoism or what is commonly called self-ishness.

Were every human being suddenly to lose that notion—which we know to be unfounded and quite unreal—all these evils, indeed all "evil," would automatically cease to exist.

That is theoretical: we know of no means of bringing that about, and it would be the famous millennium. Only an infinitesimal minority of "individuals" have succeeded in realising that they are not such. But is there any reason why the upbringing and normal education of every child should not be directed, indeed consecrated to that end?

Such a process would not produce a millenium created by self-less men and women? No, it would not, but in whatever degree it succeeded in weakening the notion of "self," the preoccupation with "self," to just that degree would life on Earth come to resemble the kingdom of Heaven.

14 ⌐ I Am Not

The Negative Path

The Buddha alone seems explicitly to have preached the doctrine which declares that the universal presence knows no I. Here the impersonality of pure consciousness, inaccessible to the process of identification, represents the plenitude of the void.

The innovation hereby involved lay in avoidance of the intrusion of the I-concept, which occurs elsewhere every time ultimate reality is identified with Atma or I-Reality. Both visions are true vision, but that of the Buddha obviates an immense obstacle.

The words "I am not" are senseless. Is this not a clear intimation that they should be true?

Pure consciousness is, is what is, nothing else is—so I am not.

When we shall have digested that may we not hope that at last we shall find that indeed we are not?

Having searched for the truth in the guise of "I Am," perhaps we shall find it in the guise of "I Am Not."

We have said that *we* are *it,* but we cannot be it—for there are no we. We have said that *it* is *we,* but it cannot be—for the same reason. There being no we, there is only it, unknown to itself. Nor can it be—for there is no thing. That must be why it is called the void, and the void must be void just because nothing is and there is no one to be.

And the universal presence is at the same time a universal absence—for there is nothing to be present and nowhere for a presence to be.

15 ·~ Perception

A perceiv*ing* is in itself pure, i.e. impersonal and real. The interpretation that follows introduces subject and object, and the result is a concept that is unreal.

That is why there is no perceiver, nothing perceived, and only the perceiving really is. It is a manifestation of pure consciousness.

Thisness

All "things" and all sentiments are interpretations only, and interpretations cannot be real in any sense.

If this is understood with insight it becomes clear that only mind *is,* that it is an impersonal non-entity, and that whoever is conscious of this is this and nothing else.

"Reality" Is Necessarily Intemporal

Any object of perception appears as a reality in Time, but since there was a period before it existed and there will be, or is now, a period in which it has ceased to exist, it cannot be a "reality."

This demonstrates that what is real in Time is unreal in Intemporality, or, as we more categorically see it, the object is not real at all.

There is, no doubt, nothing whatever that is "real" in Time.

Isness

Non-manifestation is isness. Manifestation is isness objectified by an apparent subject that is itself an object. This, we, as that pseudo-subject, can recognise as one kind of that which we know as a dream.

Knowing, understanding this, we should find ourselves abolished—so that the dream should vanish, and only non-manifestation, timeless and immutable, remain.

Milarepa Too

" . . . to discover the non-existence of the personal ego and, therefore, the fallacy of the popular idea that it existeth . . . In realising the non-existence of the personal ego the mind must be kept in quiescence."

" . . . to subdue the illusion of belief in a personal ego . . . "

16 ·- Vertical Vision, 1

Phenomenal life, the waking dream, may be said to take place on a plane surface—not as it is visually perceived but temporally. On that plane surface every action is followed by its reaction, every cause by its effect: this is the world of *karma*, of the force of circumstances, and is what we know as our life.

But an awakened sage lives and thinks vertically. If his body is flowing horizontally in the stream of time like the rest of mankind, his mind has acquired the vertical dimension which rises at right-angles from each moment of that time-river. While B hits A because A has hit B, tic-toc, the sage has no such reaction, and knows no occasion for such automatic reflex—for, from the vertical dimension, the height from which he perceives, he sees not each moment's incident but the whole picture stretched out before him. He may ignore the blow, or he may turn the other cheek for the striker's sake, but the detachment of his vision will admit of no reaction. Perceiving the preceding circumstances of the blow, he is free from constraint to react to it, and the chain-reaction is broken.

To A and the rest of mankind, the sage's inaction is unaccountable, foolish or contemptible, though a few may regard it as wise. In fact it is none of those things: it is the exercise of a freedom which he alone can have.

Vertical vision is a consequence, not a method. It cannot be practised. But the understanding of it, its being envisaged, may point towards the state of wisdom from which it will result.

17 ·~ Golden Silence

The faculty that distinguishes man from all other animals is that of speech, and he makes use of it with the enthusiasm of a convert and the lack of moderation of a child with a new toy. The popular notion of government, at all levels, is government by talking, and often it amounts to little else. The inefficiency of this is demonstrated by the fact that when obvious security is at stake, as in the case of ships at sea and armies on land, government by talking is abandoned and there is substituted for it the rule of one man, whose word is law and whose words of command are so brief as to ignore syntax. When it has happened that in the first enthusiasm of popular revolutions that natural law has been temporarily abrogated the ship has been known to sink and the army to be beaten.

It is instructive, and also entertaining, to observe that one of man's methods of showing respect, on the death of a celebrated individual or in commemoration of a catastrophe, is to observe one minute, or even two, of silence, that is to refrain from talking for that all too brief period; and that has been apt to prove too great a strain for regular application. It would appear that the maintenance of silence is well-nigh insupportable to the average man, and at the same time he cherishes an illusory notion that almost anything can be achieved by chatter. Verbiage is his primary occupation, and his method of self-assertion, and in many countries even a musical programme on the radio rarely lasts for more than a few minutes without being interrupted by an outburst of entirely superfluous "gab." "Gab," in short, is his idea of living, and he expresses his ideas, even the most erudite, with the exception of higher mathematics, in the greatest possible number of words instead of in the fewest.

But talking is probably the greatest hindrance to the development of man's spiritual possibilities, and of all forms of activity the one which most efficiently bars his way to that higher state of consciousness which is his unique possibility, his right, and his only certain justification. This is hardly an original observation; the Ch'an masters evidently knew it—since they spoke so briefly as to be barely comprehensible, and the most vital sutras, shorn of subsequent repetition, give their message in a few lines. The fact is recognised in Christianity by the Trappists and in India yogis impose on themselves long periods of silence, and, when abroad, single days at stated periods.

This need not be taken to mean that even the most serious occidentals who follow the urge towards enlightenment should abandon speech. In the course of every twenty-four hours one-third is already devoted to silence, but they might perhaps realise that chatter is not only a hindrance, as has been pointed out, but is quite clearly a psychological mechanism of defence against progress on that path on the part of the *skandha*-impulses operating in collaboration with the I-concept developed by the phenomenal "individual." It is neither difficult nor rare to be able to observe that mechanism in operation, and in such cases at least mental discipline, as it is called, is necessary, though the element of discipline should be merely a result, the result of understanding and observing that mechanism at work. This understanding need in no way hinder communication of ideas, of all kinds of interesting observations, of humour, even of gossip—for there are sixteen hours available for all that as well as for periods of silence. Perhaps there need not even be anything so formal as periods of silence, but just an abandonment of absolutely superfluous "gab"?

18 ⁓ Débris, 1

Subjectivity is what is left when all objects are ignored. Why? Because that is the process of resolving subject-object into Pure Consciousness.

People who lecture are pseudo-*jivan-muktas*. If they do not represent the I-concept posing as the Self, why would they do it? If they did not give that impression, why would people go and listen to them?

This does not apply to answering questions, nor to private conversation—which be just the interpretation of the words of the Masters. Pseudo-*éveillés* cannot fail to mislead, however "good" their intentions. These are hard words, for the intentions are probably nearly always "good," but if there is truth in them—is it not necessary to point it out?

∝

Realisation is a matter of *becoming conscious* of that which is already realised.

∝

Split-mind is composed of thoughts, and does not otherwise exist. Whole-mind is devoid of thoughts, and is "real." Therefore the splitting of the mind must be the division into two-sided thoughts, for whole-mind is the source of thoughts.

∝

It is not the eye that sees, it is not the ear that hears: there is seeing, there is hearing. Who sees? Who hears? *No one.* That is the truth. For the seeing and the seen, the hearing and the heard are impersonality, impersonal consciousness.

∝

The Cross-Roads

"Reality" (Self in Vedanta) is your ever-present consciousness.

ॐ

The space-time continuum is mind—mind in manifestation, not pure consciousness—static mind, let us say, whose counterpart is the dynamic aspect we recognise as thought. Matter is probably not different from its matrix—the space-time continuum.

ॐ

If Bhagavan[1] is the Self, we too are Bhagavan and Bhagavan is us. His words are ours; listening to him we ourselves are speaking. He appears to be without (far away in space and time), but he is also within (like any *Guru*). He is no entity. I am no entity. We are no entity: we are Unself. There is only one—and we are that. Each of us is all, and all are one. There is only one Self, and we are all (each) that.

ॐ

The explanation of Maharshi's teaching, "Who am I?," focuses split-mind on its subject, i.e. whole-mind, impersonal subjectivity, the Father, and so transcends the duality of split-mind (subject-object). "Who am I?" is not just an intellectual exercise, as has been thought, but a technique for resolving the basic dualism which bars the way to synthesis.

---

[1] *Ed. note:* Bhagavan Sri Ramana Maharshi. WWW also often refers to him as "Maharshi" or "The Maharshi."

Realization

A man who is seeking for realization is not only going round searching for his spectacles without realizing they are on his nose all the time, but also were he not actually looking through them he would not be able to see what he is looking for!

His only trouble is not knowing that they are there, and that alone hinders him from looking in the right direction. But the right direction is not without, for realization can never be an object of vision. The spectacles in question are mirrors that reflect the subject that is looking for itself.

❦

It is probably an error, and a fundamental error, to seek the resolution of each pair of opposites in some third quality or "thing." There is only a common factor behind all relative interpretations.

In doing as we do we are still subject to the notion that "things" with names really *are!* But there are no two "things," and there is no third "thing"—just a common factor, or background, *which* is *"real."*

❦

Perhaps a fifth dimension of space, or the notion of multiple dimensions beyond those we know and can use, plus time, are vague hypotheses, laboratory instruments that are better discarded? Would it not be more accurate to envisage not further directions of measurement, which we are not able to conceive, but a permanent substratum that is common to the dimensions we actually use, on to which transient images are projected, a continuum transcending, permeating and enveloping them, a continuum that itself is "real"?

❦

The universe is not real in itself, but only as a projection of underlying "reality." Phenomena are real as projections on to the "screen" of "reality."

PART II

The Negative Way

❧

The being
Of separate beings
Is non-separate being

—CHUANG-TSE

19 ·~ Ne Plus Ultra

It is necessary to understand that I Am,
In order that I may know that I Am Not,
So that, at last, I may realize that
I Am Not, therefore I Am.

20 ·~ Why Lazarus Is Still Laughing...

It may seem to be impossible to dispose of the notion "I am."
It is like a cork. The moment one ceases to hold it down up
it pops, and anyhow—who holds it down? One may say that
there is only the void, but then there is the void and the sayer
that there is only the void, which is a duality. And if one says
that the void is I, then I am also the void. Therefore I still
(objectively) am.

Quite evidently the inexistence of "I" cannot be said. But
can it be thought? That which is normally meant by thought
is potentially capable of verbal expression, so that it cannot be
thought either.

What is "I" if it is not a presence? I am a presence, if anything. But where there is a presence there can be an absence.
Therefore if I am a presence I can also be an absence. But
then, of course, an absence implies a presence. An absence is
also a presence, a presence an absence, and "I" am not-I, and
"Not-I" am I. Non-existence implies existence, so that I cannot not exist without existing. No, I cannot be disposed of,
for in disposing of me my existence is thereby posed. I am a
concept, and all concepts are dualistic, so that my inexistence
cannot be thought.

But to conclude from that dualistic analysis that I necessarily am in reality would be unwarranted. Dualistically I inevitably am, but, it seems to me, non-dualistically, and equally inevitably, that I cannot possibly be. The mere fact that dualistically I must be proves that non-dualistically I cannot be.

Have we not succeeded in establishing something that cannot be established in any other way? Manifestation is a manifestation of non-manifestation, and non-manifestation is a non-manifestation of manifestation: there cannot not be manifestation dualistically, and for that reason in reality there cannot be manifestation. So that is why "from the beginning not a thing is" (Hui Neng). Neither thing nor entity, neither world nor I. The world is my concept, built of sense-perceptions: no concepts can be real. I am a concept, built of sense-perceptions: I cannot be real.

That, surely, is the whole truth? Conceptually I must be, and via me the world must be. But beyond conceptualism nothing is, and that is the void. The void is also a non-void, or a plenum, in so far as it is a concept. There is just absolutely nothing that can be said about this. But it can be cognised, by cognition that is definitely beyond thought. Trying to say it, trying to make it a concept is futile.

So what can we do? When the notion that I am comes to me—I can still laugh.

Having laughed at the notion that I am—and indeed it is far funnier, because more absurd, than the notion that I am not, which raised a good laugh when one first noticed it—what then? Conceptually I am, and how. Supra-conceptually there is laughter. Which do I choose? There is no choosing. I am and I am not—as long as I live.

21 ·— The Illuminating Vision

The fact of conceiving that which is expressed by the words "I am" makes "that I am" an object of the conceiving subject. Ultimately, it seems, I am necessarily an object. In fact a subject is necessarily an object in so far as it is seen as a subject.

What, then, is the subject of which I am the object? There is only one subject that cannot become an object, because it cannot be conceived and has no existence in duality—and that is "I am not."

And that, no doubt, is why "I am not, therefore I am." It is also why I cannot possibly be, because, in order to be, I must become an object—and because I cannot be that, I am not. And why, not being, yet I am.

Subject and object are then seen as one. We are both subject and object, alternatively in duality, simultaneously, fused, in unicity.

And is not that the "Truth of Ch'an"—as Huang Po assured us?

❦

If Being is subject, and everything, including myself (in the dream) is object, then I am object, and subject only in so far as I am Being, like everything else. But Being is also an object and is not.

❦

Because I am not—everything is.
Because I am—not a thing is.
Everything is, because Now (the now-moment) is always present.

❧

When subject becomes object, object thereby becomes subject. For each is both, and both are each.

❧

But neither I-object nor I-subject, but only I-am-not can see subject and object as one.

22 ·~ *Irreverence*

The Buddha was sometimes naughty, but he may have done it to tease. For instance he was fond of saying that *Nirvana* is the same as *Samsara*. That is ridiculous or obvious according to where you happen to be standing.

Hui Neng was more downright— but then he was a young peasant. When someone asked him whether it was the pennant that flapped, or the wind, he replied quite frankly that it was the man's own mind that was flapping.

As for the Buddha's little jest, the answer is equally obvious and, in fact, the same. Where split-mind sees *Samsara*, whole-mind sees *Nirvana*. And they themselves are only the same in so far as neither of them exists—as he would have been the first to admit, and, no doubt, often pointed out after enunciating a doctrine about them.

No wonder the monks burnt his images when they were feeling cold and were short of fuel?

23 · Baubles of the Mind (Sutras and the Void)

The philosophers of the early centuries of this era who put their sutras into the mouth of the Buddha seem to us to have rendered them as incomprehensible as words could make them. If they did it in order to confuse the likes of us—they succeeded magisterially.

In the Diamond Sutra they speak of *Samsara* and *Nirvana* as being identical. In the Heart Sutra they go further; they speak of form, and the other disparate *skandhas,* then the Chain of Causation, and finally the Four Holy Truths, in fact all *dharmas,* and declare them to be identical with Emptiness, and Emptiness to be identical with them, and in every possible way and from every possible point of view. In short they point out that all *dharmas* are void.

But these *dharmas* are all concepts, baubles of the mind, and they treat them solemnly as though they existed in their own right and were "things" solidly and indubitably existing. Then they proceed to state the contrary, and finally, with a double somersault, the contrary of the contrary. At first sight this looks like a precursor of the ko-an technique that developed some five centuries later in Japan.

Yet without all these gymnastics the doctrine appears to be quite clear and simple and obvious, and I think it must appear so in the light of the later T'ang masters whose teaching was largely based upon these sutras and the Lanka. All these *dharmas* are just concepts, perfectly inexistent, and are interpretations by divided mind of that which whole-mind knows as what we call a void. The one perceives the world of multiplicity and phenomena in space and time; the other knows emptiness (though it is divided mind that so calls it) and noumenon. Evidently they are the same—but their identity lies in the mind, not in the contrary interpretations that are "perceived," for the apparent difference depends on which eye is looking at them.

What advantage can there be, one may ask, in trying to see contraries as identical, with the eye that can only see contraries? One can only suppose that it was a technique devised in order to prise open the other eye so that both contraries could be seen and recognised as one whole, and the contraries of contraries and their contraries, and so on *ad infinitum*.

I wonder if all this is necessary for us, and whether it could possibly be efficacious—for contraries cannot be seen as identical by the reasoning mind whose *modus operandi* is a function of its inherent duality, so that it is not possible, whatever anyone may think or pretend, to "see" *Samsara* and *Nirvana* as identical, for no two separate thoughts can ever occur simultaneously. Such "identity" as can be apprehended by reasoning is not such, but only a reasoned assimilation of two different things that are seen to resemble one another. *Identity is quite other.* It is an act of direct vision on the part of whole-mind.

24 ·– Ultimate and Unconditioned "Reality" Is Negative and Void

Let us be clear about this and express it in our occidental manner of speech, and try to see what exactly is this idea of a void—for it is an idea like any other.

The phenomenal, objective, relative world of sense-impressions is an interpretation by divided and reasoning mind (which operates by a comparison of opposites) of noumenon, the absolute, subject, none of which (if you regard them as different in any way or as aspects of one whole) it is able directly to perceive. And the contrary, with which everything here in question is to be identified, is called Emptiness. As the Void it is the counterpart of Plenum, and all these qualities, these *dharmas,* treated as though they were "things," are therefore elements in that plenitude. A void, however, is a total negative. If you think of Reality or Being, as you are taught to do, you are assuming something positive, and each of these positives is inevitably accompanied by its negative, which we have to term Non-reality and Non-being. It is this negative that is the Void or Emptiness, and that negative implies its constituent plenum, so that this Void, being that which is not, is also that which appears to be, i.e. Non-manifestation manifested—which is the phenomenal and apparent universe or *Samsara.*

This surely is the real message of these sutras—that our intuition must apprehend the negative reality of the Void in order to comprehend that its positive element is Appearance, and that thus, *and not the other way round,* must they be seen if their identity is to be assimilated and not merely assumed.

Note: Re *dharmas,* "Their true nature is a no-nature, and their no-nature is their true nature; for all *dharmas* have one mark only, i.e. no mark... for there are not two natures of *dharma,* but just one single is the nature of all *dharmas.* And the true nature of all *dharmas* is a no-nature, and their no-nature is their true nature. It is thus that all points of possible attachment are abandoned." (Prajnaparamita Sutra, cited by Dr. Edward Conze in his *Diamond Sutra,* p. 36.)

"This *Dharma,* i.e. the ultimate reality in both its objective and subjective form...." (Op. cit., p. 37.)

The "real" nature of all manifestation is *no-nature,* and of all ideas of "reality" and of being—for all such are concepts or *dharmas.* They are directly negative or void, and only indirectly positive and relative.

25 ⌣ *Nothing in Something*

To look upon the Void as an emptiness that exists somewhere in a cosmic fullness will never open the mind to its wholeness. Vision must start afresh by realizing that a cosmic plenitude is an imaginary implication, and that the cosmos itself is not. The Void is not nothing somewhere within something: that something is nothing, there is nowhere within it, and the Void is that.

Something in Nothing

It is the basic notion, the fundamental conception that is erroneous. People start by assuming reality, a something, a positively existing continuum, and then seek to situate the Void somewhere therein. But it is the Void we have to take as the basic notion, the fundamental conception, the continuum that is a non-continuum—and then see that if there is anything apparent anywhere it can only be in that.

That Which Is Not, 1

We must go further! Just as we have realized that "I am not in reality," and that there is no being therein, so we have to understand that there is no reality either.

Reality is just a manifestation of No-reality, for only nothing can be said to exist. In fact, of course, nothing exists, which means that it does not exist as nothing.

That again is the Void, directly approached or seen as it is not.

I am Not

That which I think is "I am" is really nothing of the kind: that is that-which-*Is*—experience, consciousness, being. I am not any of those things, or all of them, for no such thing as I exists. "I" is only a technique whereby experience is registered in a manner that is interpreted as "personal."

That which I think is "I am" is experience, consciousness, being, but *they* are not either except in so far as they are not.

They are not, therefore they are. For so it is.

26 ⁓ The Ultimate Understanding

The essential understanding is that in reality nothing is. This is so obvious that it is not perceived. We quote Hui Neng's "From the beginning not a thing is" without apprehending its full significance. We refer to the Void and Emptiness without realizing what is implied. What is meant is just what is said, i.e. that nothing is—that Nothing alone is what is, not that no thing is real in Something, not that in positive Being, which we tacitly assume, no object is real. Positive Being is not to be assumed, but negative Being—Non-being. It is non-being only that is, and there is nothing but that. It is only in function of Non-being that being *seems to be*.

Non-being is; and it is because Non-being is, and only Non-being, that any being can be, for being is a manifestation of Non-being.

The Realization of the Void

Being must be replaced by Non-being—in order that anything may be.

For Being is a projection of Non-being.

This is the necessary realization, and, perhaps, the ultimate—that Nothing alone is, that there is only Is-not, that Is
is only by virtue of Is-not—for nothing but Nothing is of
itself, and only the isness of Is-not can be.

That is the realization of the Void.

Note: This is the deep meaning of the Buddha's words in the
Diamond Sutra about Bodhisattvas knowing no Being, and of Hui
Neng's declaration that we must rid ourselves of the idea of Being
as well as of self. Its meaning has been masked by the article "a"
usually given it elsewhere, which appears to assimilate it to a term
for self, ego, individual, whereas it is to be applied to the plane of
"reality."

The Void (Non-Being) alone is complete.

27 ⁓ Because It Is Not . . .

Authority is comforting: let us seek it. In Chapter 13 of the
Diamond Sutra the Buddha takes a series of five examples—
transcendental wisdom, his own teaching, particles of dust,
the world-system, and the thirty-two marks of a superman.
Of each of these it is said that they are, that they are not, and
that therefore they are. For instance, "Because what was
taught as particles of dust by the Tathagata, as no particles
that was taught by the Tathagata. Therefore they are called
"particles of dust." And this world-system the Tathagata
has taught as no world-system. Therefore is it called a
world-system." And so on for each.

This is followed by one of the elaborate hyperbolic
metaphors used to emphasise the supreme importance of this
teaching. And indeed the Venerable Subhuti is moved to
tears thereby, and according to Mr. A. F. Price's translation

from the Chinese, had "an interior realization" of its meaning. One might read this many times without understanding the tremendous importance attached to it, for neither translator draws attention to it or offers an explanation.

Nevertheless its supreme importance is evident enough when one understands that each of these contradictions is just an example of the formula "It is: because it is not, therefore it is," or, as I give it, "I (apparently) am: because I am not, therefore I am," or "Because Reality is Non-reality, therefore it is Reality," "Since Being is Non-being, therefore it is Being."

The importance of this understanding of the precedence of the negative element to the positive, of the Void to the Plenum, of Non-being to Being, of I am not to I am, is sufficiently great to justify any degree of hyperbole—for it requires a reversal of our habitual way of regarding these matters, and a transvaluation of our established values according to which, as I have pointed out, we assume positive Reality or Being and then look for their negatives. That is, we imagine the Void as an emptiness in a pre-existing fullness, a nothing in an assumed Something, whereas we are urgently required to apprehend the ubiquitous pre-existence of Nothing out of which something may appear, or out of Non-manifestation manifestation.

In the following chapter, 14, Subhuti, full of enthusiasm, says, "Through it cognition has been produced in me. Not have I ever before heard such a discourse on *Dharma*. Most wonderfully blest will be those who, when this sutra is being taught, will produce a true perception. And that which is true perception, *that indeed is no perception*. Therefore the Tathagata teaches true perception." And again, in the same chapter, "This perception of a being, Subhuti, that is just a non-perception. Those all-beings of whom the Tathagata has spoken, they are indeed no-beings." And why? Bec Tathagata speaks *in accordance with reality.*" (Dr. Edward Conze, "The Diamond Sutra.")

"In accordance with reality" means in our vocabulary—since the term "reality" is so variously understood—"in accordance with whole-mind."

It might not be too much to say that this, together with its counterpart the inexistence of any kind of self, is the *lietmotiv* of this sutra, capital in gnostic Buddhism, and constitutes perhaps its essential message. Subsequently indeed a considerably greater number of other "dharmas" are treated according to the same formula, one of the most direct of which is, " 'Beings, beings', Subhuti, the Tathagata has taught that they are all no-beings. Therefore has he spoken of 'all beings.' " (Ch. 21)

⚘

It might be thought that what is meant is "I am and I am not, and only in that sense I am," but the words of the Buddha are very definite and are reiterated *ad nauseam* in the Hindu manner. He *taught* that things and concepts *(dharmas)* are, then he *taught* that things and concepts *(dharmas)* are not, and that is *why* things and concepts *(dharmas)* are.

But Vedanta Advaita teaches "I am," and the Buddhist doctrine of the Void teaches "I am not." The Buddha makes it clear, again and again, that it is *on account of this latter teaching* that in a sense I can be.

It therefore seems apparent that there are three stages on this path. The pilgrim learns to *understand* that he is, after having understood that as an I-concept he is not. Then, and only then, he comes to *know* that nevertheless he is not, for nothing is, not even he. And finally he *realizes* that in consequence of that and in a sense inconceivable before, he is.

Hence the formula: I am: I am not, therefore I am.

ॐ

The essential doctrine of the Diamond Sutra is that no sort or kind of self is to be considered as existing. Having disposed of the I-concept, the Buddha proceeds to dispose of the elements that serve as a basis for it, i.e. the five *skandhas,* and, finally, of all "dharmas" from the supreme doctrine of enlightenment, via all perceptions and the Four Holy Truths (the Heart Sutra here) down to his own physical body.

In short, as Hui Neng realized so early in life, nothing at all exists, which is the Void. But the Buddha always adds that therefore everything exists in some manner. The translations are unsatisfactory here, for some say "are said to exist" or "are called such and such," whereas others are less evasive. One may suspect that none quite gives the sense.

28 ·- Néant

The current theories to the effect that the Void does not in fact mean what it says, that it is not emptiness, is not nothing but is only emptiness *of* something, imply that it *is* something, and moreover something in something.

Surely this is shirking the truth: it is everything we think we know, therefore it must be nothing we know. It is Nothing, therefore everything is. *Were it anything there could not be anything.* It is precisely because it is Nothing that there can be anything. Either one sees this or one does not: it is evident, but it cannot be proved.

"Form is emptiness," says the Heart Sutra (the Heart of the Prajna-paramita), "and emptiness is form." Then it explains: "Emptiness is *nothing but* form, and form is *nothing but* emptiness." Finally it completes the definition by adding: "Apart from emptiness there is no form, and apart from form there is no emptiness." In other words: "Apart from nothing there is no anything, and apart from anything there is no nothing." Or again, "Apart from our phenomenal world there is no Void, and apart from the Void there is no phenomenal world."

The Void then is nothing, absolutely nothing—and Nothing is absolutely everything. For both exist only in mind.

All talk about the Void being this and that, not meaning that and the other, is not only balking the issue—it is shutting oneself off from the truth. It is necessary to realize that the Void means exactly Nothing, and that exactly Nothing is all that there is. And that that is the reason why anything can appear to be. Otherwise one has the whole situation the wrong way round, for one continues to think that reality is positive, something positively existing, of which the negative is inconceivable. *But reality itself is negative*, and its positive is just appearance, and both are concepts of the split or *samsaric* mind. In whole-mind reality is neither positive nor negative—*for there is nothing of the kind*. Reality simply IS NOT.

This seems to be the Essential Doctrine of the Prajna-paramita, revealing the illusion which constitutes the bondage of *Samsara*, the barrier which prevents mind from knowing itself as no-mind, pure negativity or the absolute unconscious.

29 ⸱– The Photographic Image Also Is Negative

The Void only appears to be Emptiness or Nothing when it is regarded as the opposite of Something or Everything. Or it is only when Non-being is seen as the counterpart of Being that it appears as Nothing.

But when Something or Everything is seen as the counterpart of Nothing—then Nothing becomes Everything, and Non-being can be seen as Being.

30 ⸱– Discrimination

"When discrimination is not discriminating and yet discriminating, we have perfect enlightenment." (Suzuki, *The Essentials of Zen Buddhism*, p. 22). This seems to mean: when the kind of discrimination in question is not a discriminating (does not discriminate or is not seen as discriminating) and yet discriminates in some sense, we have perfect enlightenment, i.e. either perfect enlightenment is necessary in order to do that, or when we are able to do that we experience perfect enlightenment. But what is the meaning of this?

Dr. Suzuki speaks on the next page of the "pure undefiled spiritual world of non-discrimination, while the defiling world is that of thought and discrimination." We may then re-define the statement as follows: "When discrimination, based on rational thinking, is seen to be really non-discriminating, i.e. not a discriminating at all *in reality,* it is then seen to be nevertheless what we know as discriminating, but of a kind only recognisable as such by those who have perfect enlightenment, i.e. who have seen that rational thinking, in the spiritual world of reality, is not discrimination at all."

The Negative Way

In our own jargon: what our two eyes see and split-mind knows as rational discrimination, our third eye sees and whole-mind knows undiscriminated as one whole, but when thereafter we see it—let us say with all three eyes—we perceive the discrimination that potentially exists in not discriminating, in perceiving that one whole wherein there is no place for discrimination when seen by the intuitional eye. The discriminating then effected by our normal two eyes and split-mind is of another character, one which we may provisionally describe as "potential."

More precisely, in whole-mind the discrimination of split-mind is automatically merged in not discriminating, although potential discriminating is inherent therein, so that in the enlightened the two points of view can be seen, the discrimination of split-mind tempered by the not discriminating vision of whole-mind.

Note: I have adhered throughout to the distribution of the terms "discrimination" and "discriminating" as used by Dr. Suzuki.

In this, unusually, a Zen master speaks of discriminating—which is that which occurs in the mind, instead of that which is discriminated—which is the apparent object of that process. Habitually we are asked to see two discriminated objects as one, two "opposites" or complementaries united in what is termed "self-identity." But there are no such objects, as they well know, outside consciousness, and the functioning of split-mind whose *modus operandi* lies in dualistic alternation in a time-sequence, is not capable of having two thoughts simultaneously. The requirement of the masters only appears to be feasible when it is replaced in the mind wherein it occurs, and therein, as here, we can see at least how it may be.

This constitutes a key-example of the Buddha's formula, quoted from the Diamond Sutra, for the term "discriminating" covers all forms of judging, and the innumerable qualities and things judged by us are not considered, but the *mental process* only—which is all that can be said to occur or to have any degree of reality.

31 ·- A.B.C. 1: The Culprit

All the evil in the world, and all the unhappiness, comes from the I-concept.

There are two methods of dealing with it: the dualistic approach, by seeking to discipline, purify, or otherwise ameliorate this supposed self which suffers and does ill, that is working by means of that which is itself the cause; and the non-dualist method, by disposing of it, by eradicating the cause, by realizing that it is only a concept and is not I at all.

Only the second method can be completely efficacious, because it alone is radical and permanent. If it can be realized that the subject is not the I-concept, that the I-concept is not the subject, its power—for evil as for suffering—must automatically cease to be effective.

છે

We do not possess an "ego."
We are possessed by the idea of one.

છે

32 ⁓ A.B.C. 2: Transvaluation of Values

We think of insides as being the insides of outsides—for it is only outsides that we know, and even what we speak of as insides are themselves only outsides within other outsides.

If we understood, we should see things the other way round, for the within is nearer reality than the without. Everything we know should be the without of a *within*, the external *appearance* of something real and unseen within, "behind" or "beneath" it.

This is an aspect of the realization that negative, not positive, is fundamental.

Moreover we think of ourselves as outsides—women more uninterruptedly than men—and "inside" is to us either an organ (itself another outside) or something mental. There we approach the truth—but like a moth trying to light on a candle-flame.

If we firmly transvalued our values and thought of ourselves as withins, and *only* as withins—withouts being merely symbols thereof—we should be at least on the road that leads in the direction of understanding.

33 ⁓ A.B.C. 3: The Buddha's Formula in Relative Reality

It may be possible to understand the Buddha's formula more readily by means of an example based on phenomenal existence.

Take any object—say a jug—and let it represent, be a symbol for, reality. If you then photograph it you have a negative representation of it in two dimensions, composed merely of light and shade. The positive reproduction of that symbol reverses the light and shade, and reveals an image which we can recognise as that of what we know as a jug. An animal, unable to form concepts, cannot normally recognise the object, but sees only light and shade.

That, in fact, is the Buddha's formula, in reverse. The positive image is that which appears to be in phenomenal existence. The negative image is the background of that, its relative reality from which it derives, that which precedes it and without which it cannot be. But both are just two-dimensional images composed of light and shade, quite illusory, unrecognisable except by beings who use concepts— just representations of the jug-reality whose existence is in a further dimension.

So you have the formula exactly: it is (as an appearance); it is not (is a negative): therefore that which is represented (and is real) alone is.

Note 1: We notice in passing that this example reveals clearly the three degrees of perception available to man: perception of "reality," known only to the awakened; perception of "relative reality," the objective world known to us; perception of images and symbols by means of conceptualisation. The first is real; the second is a representation of the real; the third is imaginary. The Buddha's formula treats of the two first forms of perception; our example is applied to the two latter.

Note 2: The photographic apparatus represents the sensorial apparatus by means of which we interpret, or create, the apparent world which surrounds us.

34 ·- *The Buddha, Original, or Self Nature*

This "real nature" with whose revelation the Ch'an Masters are primarily concerned, or the Atman-"I" of the Vedantists, is not the far-off, unreachable will-o'-the-wisp we are apt to imagine, but just the within of which we know the without. It is just the other side of the medal, and it lies wherever our senses and our intellect cease to function.

At that point it is to be found, and that "point" is in every direction, so that wherever we turn we cannot avoid it. Nor, of course, is it a long way off. It is not "off" at all: it is within, here and now, and where we are before we start to look for it. We don't have to look for it, nor could we ever see it by looking. By the absence of looking, listening, touching, tasting, smelling, and thinking we realize that we are it. For it is the unmanifest of that which we see, hear, feel, taste, smell, and think of as manifest. It is the negative of everything that is positive to us, the reality of every illusion—and every sensory and conceptual experience is an illusion. I have only to cease to be in order to become that which an I is, to realize that I am not in order to be That I Am.

Where our sensory and intellectual experience ceases, where we can no longer know anything by their means, there lies what to them can only be Nothing or the Void—that is our "real nature," that is pure consciousness which is all that is, and it is just that.

Put in another manner, it is just the underside of the surfaces which are all that we are aware of anywhere or in anything, the within of the without which surrounds us on all sides, the back of the front. It is the Unmanifest from within which everything manifests, the Not-I which is all the I that is.

35 ·~ Alter-Egoism

A Causerie

Deliberate "altruism" has no spiritual value, for it is at the same time, and inevitably, a reinforcement of the I-complex and therefore also deliberate "egoism." "One" and "other" are two aspects of one concept, and that concept is the barrier between us and universal consciousness.

And yet we think that an awakened sage serves others, and we feel that we should imitate him? But he does it precisely because there is no longer for him a "one," and therefore there are for him no longer "others" either. He does not, in fact, serve others—for he has transcended both other and one. He just serves—for that is his inevitable way of living while still in manifestation.

Nor is imitation of any use. But if we cease to think of our "selves" we shall automatically be considerate to "others," and in the degree in which we loosen the bonds of our sempiternal egoism, in that same degree shall we be seen to act in a manner that is interpreted as altruistic. We ourselves shall be unconscious of that—for otherwise our bonds would not have been loosened—and that is the only kind of "altruism" that matters. Like so much else, care for others, that is absence of care for ourselves, is a result and not a method.

Is someone murmuring something about "love"? There is no such thing as "love" in reality. What we seek to describe by that word is emotion experienced in certain highly personal channels, charged with possessiveness, shadowed by jealousy, with its counterpart "hate" ever ready to take its place. Sages do not love or hate: they only know pure-affectivity, which does not pass through egoistic channels and which cannot be interpreted at all. From our viewpoint we may mistake that for love, but such is an elementary failure to understand. Sages cannot know love-hate, for that is affectivity polluted by an I-concept. Affectivity, however, in its pure state, as *karuna*, looks to us like a singularly purified kind of love, sometimes even called "divine." In a sense it is that—though the description is inaccurate and topsy-turvy, since it is "love" that is, in fact, a polluted kind of affectivity.

So what can we do? We can only follow the negative path that opens our "third" eye to the fact that we are not and that nothing is. Then, and only then, we shall find out that, in the new sense or dimension in which everything is, we are that. Then "other" and "one" will indeed be inconceivable, for nowhere is there place for false interpretations and everything is essentially one, since subject and object are no more.

But is there not a difference between altruism and charity? No doubt, for the latter is one application of the former. But we are not able to know whether what we give to others or do for them is ultimately beneficent or maleficent whatever be the appearances and our intentions. The relief of suffering? Yes, yes, but should we not make it our own before we relieve it? In so-doing we identify ourselves with other-than-I, and that is a step towards universality of consciousness.

The doctrine of the sages seems clear on this matter and, here at least, easy to understand: the only real service we can render to that which we perceive and interpret in phenomenal existence as "others" is by awakening to universal consciousness ourselves. That is not in order that we may preach to them from a comprehension that cannot be expressed in the verbal symbols of dualistic thought, though they can be helped somewhat in that way, but because in the awakened state universal consciousness can be made accessible to men via the medium of the awakened in an immense sensorially-imperceptible radiation that is not subject to time, to space, or to any of the limitations of our tri-dimensional interpretation of "Reality." Besides this the power of words is negligible, and its scope and penetration are limited only by the degree of receptivity encountered in men themselves.

Note: The separateness of each of us that is so apparent to our tri-dimensional interpretive faculty is a superficial appearance. The persona—as its name implies—is a mask, and a fugitive, illusory one at that, whereas the universal "reality" "behind" or "beneath" it is ubiquitous. Our individual appearances are just ripples forming and dissolving on the surface of an ocean that encircles the cosmos. Only the I-notion prevents us from perceiving that which we really are.

36 ·- Glimpses of the Bodhi-Mind?

As we follow the urge and accumulate comprehension there seems to develop within us another consciousness than the congenital one which has grown up with us as a result of psycho-somatic experience. This apparently new consciousness is nourished by intuitional apprehension and increases in power and immediacy as understanding deepens. It seems to be independent of our mundane psyche and to function in a further dimension of mind although it can manifest via our intellectual and emotional faculties. The one is subject to time and is egocentric, the other appears to be intemporal and unaffected by any evident notion of "I." As its intensity augments we suffer more acutely from the contrast between it and the I-ridden psyche by which we are still possessed. We feel ever more deeply that we are not the mundane reflection of consciousness that we are conditioned to recognise as our selves, and that we are this new consciousness in which our identity seems to disappear. Yet the stranglehold of the egocentric psyche reestablishes its possession of us every time we seek to merge our identity in the intemporal, and we long for the day, fearing it may never come, when we may cease to be possessed and can lose our selves in the universality of the consciousness which has developed "behind" and "beyond" our perennial tormentor. We feel that then we shall be it, and shall cease to be "I"; in fact we seem to know already that we are it, and that our "I" is a masquerade.

When the penetration of this transcendent consciousness is strong we tend no longer to see living things as objects, indifferent or inimical, but as part of ourselves; perhaps rather as other parts of one whole which is that nature which surrounds us all—though these somewhat different ways of apprehending do not then seem to be so different.

Within this consciousness love-hate gives place to a purer affectivity, resembling benediction-compassion, excitement-distress passes into serenity, and greed, envy, fear, pride and other forms of ego-polluted emotion are in abeyance or are represented by pure affectivity itself.

Another characteristic of this state, when awareness lays us open to it, is that its nature seems to be subject to radiation, sensorially imperceptible but recognisable by those living things that can receive it, or, if not recognisable by them, then recognisable by us as having been received—though this spatial concept may be a phenomenal interpretation of direct contact, which it seeks to describe, or even of contact with a common factor.

But have we "developed" this new consciousness; is it "new," and is it "ours" at all? Or is it something ubiquitous to which we have given formal access whereby it may possess us when it can? Could it be both, at once our own essential nature of which we have become partly conscious, and an aspect of universal mind that we have become able to apprehend, ours in so far as the phenomenon each of us is comes to recognise it as our self, and an aspect of universal mind in so far as it has become cognisable to us via our phenomenal faculties?

One thing at least we know, and cannot not know: this is more real than the I-ridden reflection of consciousness in which it is impossible for us any longer to believe, and the corollary of that, which is that nothing matters to us so much as to augment its power and immediacy so that it may take possession of us entirely and once and for all.

Yet another thing do we know, and ever more clearly, and that is the nature of the barrier which prevents us from becoming that which we now recognise that we are. That barrier stands out blatantly, and it is the conditioned belief that the psycho-somatic apparatus, which in phenomenal existence bears the name we know as ours, is our self. That alone is what holds us in bondage. Then *what is it?* A conceptual make-shift that has acquired an imaginary reality, whereas the reality behind our psycho-somatic appearance *is not* that concept? Yes, and if we can destroy that imaginary reality the conceptual make-shift that depends upon it will cease to be. Is that like drowning a man in order to cure his disease? Yes, for that man is the "old man" who must die in order that the "new man" may be born. Yes, for the totality of that pseudo-reality must be seen as no-reality, in order that "reality" may be seen—and that is the supreme message of the Tathagata in the Diamond Sutra, as has already been explained.

37 ◡ *Love: An Antidote*

Hard Words

Writers on metaphysics, even some metaphysicists, sometimes talk about love. This, surely, is great nonsense. Where
is there love? (I speak of love as we know and mean it.) As
the mosquito loves us? Yes, only like that. And as I love cake.
Where there is not jealous desire for possession, there is just
plain dislike. Tigers do not love wolves, nor slugs snails. Mice
do not love cats, nor worms birds. Sentimental people may
think they give out universal love, but the very plants they
dote on dread their touch (see Chunder Bose's experiments).
There is no place for love in the phenomenal world of nature
except as an incentive to reproduction and for protection of
the young. Love exists, yes indeed, but in normal manifestation it finds expression in its counterpart of hate.

But this should not be interpreted as a sneer at good intentions, but rather as a kick in the pants for self-deception.
What these kindly people are yearning to give is not love at
all, but a chemically pure emotion of which love is a polluted
derivation. The basic urge they have is infinitely purer than
any manifestation of love. Pure affectivity is finding access to
their consciousness and is seeking expression. If, instead of
inducing a state of psychic cirrhosis in any imaginary ego,
they were able to understand this, their affectivity should
manifest as compassion or as impersonal benediction, and
this radiation would render service to all forms of life in their
vicinity.

Love is an egocentric manifestation: the essential oneness
of all life has no room for love.

38 ·- *The Myth of "Mankind," 1*

TWO: Is a man who states "I love dogs" nearer to enlightenment than one who says "I hate dogs"?

ONE: I can see no difference whatever.

TWO: Why so?

ONE: In both cases an inexistence claims an inexistent emotion regarding another inexistence.

TWO: Might I not say that one half of a reality claims one half of an emotion regarding another half of a reality? And that one is the better series of halves, and the other the worse?

ONE: Three halves do not make one whole!

TWO: But in phenomenal existence is not one better?

ONE: No doubt, but you spoke of enlightenment. Neither has a foot on the lowest rung of the ladder. The former, however, might be expected to climb higher if he reached the ladder, though even that does not necessarily follow.

TWO: How is the ladder reached by either?

ONE: You know well that the difference between love and hate is one of interpretation only. The reality of both is neither—not a mixture, not both, just neither.

TWO: Most people would have thought it was both.

ONE: Alas, they would. But never can both be seen as one. Seeing them as neither creates a void, is the void if you wish, and that void, if left void, is filled by the suchness of both.

TWO: Which is...?

ONE: "A" no longer thinks he loves or hates "B": he becomes "B." One aspect of a whole does not have an emotion regarding another aspect of that which he is. He recognises himself as integral with everything that is, with all elements of the dream which he is living.

TWO: So that he and the dog are one?

ONE: It is a pity to take a domestic animal, for whom all decent people have respect and affection—even though they may not have recognised that they and that animal are mutually aspects of one another. Take, rather, the bodhisattva's vow never to accept his own reward until every blade of grass has found enlightenment. Few people are sentimental about blades of grass.

TWO: What then is the emotion regarding blades of grass?

ONE: Since only the awakened know it, and since they have no non-dualistic language they could only seek to indicate it by some such term as "pure affectivity," "compassion," "caritas"—impersonal, unpossessive, benedictive. Let us call it a distillation, and potent as a distillation is.

TWO: And is a blade of grass exactly the same to him as his personal friend—a horse or a dog or any other creature that shares his life—pardon, his "living dream"?

ONE: A lighthouse is impersonal, but when its beam falls on a specific object it illumines that object with the totality of its light.

TWO: I sense a lot behind this; switch on the lighthouse—the beam of knowledge this time.

ONE: Knowledge also is impersonal. Use your own lighthouse and tell me what you see. You have betrayed the fact that you see something behind it, beyond "this." What do you see?

TWO: That human arrogance, apparently unlimited is at the same time totally unjustified. Man has no fundamental superiority?

ONE: He knows how to form concepts. What other superiority has he?

TWO: That is a superiority like galloping faster, flying higher, having a better "nose"—relative and quite superficial. There is no hierarchy in reality?

ONE: How could there be a hierarchy in one whole? Aspects vary, but the whole remains one.

TWO: Man grossly overestimates the importance of his capacity of forming concepts. It gives him an apparent power which he abuses beyond the limits of outrage.

ONE: So it appears. But he pays. *Tout se paye.*

TWO: That is why he is unhappy?

ONE: Would it not be more accurate to say that is why he seeks happiness where no happiness can lie, why his vain search for happiness is in escape and evasion, why his idea of happiness can never be such? That is perhaps a definition of misery?

TWO: Man tends to think that nothing matters but mankind; even in metaphysics, even, perhaps, in the Scriptures he tends to think of nothing but himself?

ONE: I congratulate you on having noticed it; not everybody who should do so—does. "Mankind" is the key-stronghold of the I-concept. It too must fall.

TWO: Man must recognise himself as one absolutely with all nature, an integral part of the whole dream, and in no way fundamentally superior to any other part?

ONE: There can be no superior or inferior in the Void of Reality. That is interpretation and arrogance on the part of split-mind: it is worse than a crime—it is nonsense!

TWO: If he does realize this—what then?

The Negative Way

ONE: What happens when the phantom personage who represents you in your dreams recognises that he too is only part of the dream, and no more real than, no different from, any other part of the dream-fabric?

TWO: I'd expect to wake up!

ONE: So you would. Why? Because the dreamer would find that he is no longer dreaming.

TWO: It would be wakening to "Reality"?

ONE: How could it not be? There is no difference: two degrees of dreaming, that is all.

TWO: So it is as important as that?

ONE: I do not know if there is a hierarchy of importance, but really knowing oneself as an integral part of nature, and no more important than any other, is equivalent to knowing that one does not exist as such. When you know that you do not exist as yourself, there is no longer any barrier between that suchnesss which is all that you are and "reality" itself—for they are one. You know of it as the void, or emptiness, for that is how it must appear to you now, that is as the other side of manifestation, the behind-the-veil from which appearance, or the dream, is projected.

TWO: Is that not, then, a direct path?

ONE: I know of none better, nearer, more obvious. You have only to follow it. Incidentally it is the Negative Way.

TWO: But it is not known!

ONE: Nonsense! It is the famous and eternal *Prajna-paramita!* But you do not recognise it in so simple a guise. It is not wrapped up in oriental splendor! Tread it, old man—and why not here, now, and so?

TWO: What an ass one must be to imagine that one is apart from everything else, and pitted against everything else into the bargain, when all the time one is just an inseparable aspect of that!

ONE: Recognising that you are an ass is going straight for the truth. You are—and the ass is you also!

39 · The Myth of "Mankind," 2

TWO: I want to come back to what we were discussing last night. Have you any objection?

ONE: If you have successfully become that donkey you identified yourself with, I shall listen to you entranced.

TWO: I see this failure to understand our identity with the nature that surrounds us, with other elements of our living dream, and our lack of superiority to any element—as very serious.

ONE: It could be what is holding us back?

TWO: That is my intuition.

ONE: It may well be a heavy shackle, and one which passes unobserved. And at the same time it should open the way to a rapid understanding.

TWO: From where do we inherit this handicap? From our religion?

ONE: Yes, but not necessarily from Jesus; his recorded words are too fragmentary. He seemed to understand sparrows, but not fish; and his callousness where fig trees are concerned was total. Our factual information is not of a character that allows us to form an opinion.

TWO: The churches are to blame?

ONE: Churches are always to blame, for they attempt to represent permanence in a world whose character is incessant mutation. The early Fathers, such as St. Clement of Alexandria and Origen, were trying to develop the doctrine of Jesus, but the Nordic Fathers of the Church, fresh from Valhalla, saw that as heresy. The result is before you. Man is the centre of the universe, animals have no souls, human arrogance is an article of faith, and dualism is not phenomenal but reality. How can an upbringing based on such nonsense not be a handicap?

TWO: Yet Christians are kind to animals, real Christians, and they try to see the Almighty in Nature.

ONE: A kindly condescension is valueless, for it is dualist, and it is from an imaginary "I." Nor do animals appreciate it: they are totally uninformed concerning their inferiority, and totally unaware of their soullessness. They resent any treatment that is not as between equals. And they are right—for their only reality is identical with our own.

TWO: Can an animal be a sage?

ONE: Of course! Why ever not? Being largely sub-conceptual rather than concept-bound can hardly be a disadvantage for knowing a state which is non-conceptual! If you like to look at it from an evolutionary point of view, a human sage is on a curve of the spiral immediately above that on which an animal sage would be, but then evolution does not exist as a thing-in-itself: it exists only in the mind that uses it, i.e. it is an instrument not a reality. There is no "Time."

TWO: Is there any evidence for animal sageness?

ONE: The kind of evidence you are thinking of would not make sense. Sages like the Maharshi had the evidence of profound and incontrovertible knowledge.

He had Lakshmi[1] buried near his mother, instead of being cremated, and, when asked why, he answered nonchalantly that he was with her when she died, and that she was enlightened. If evidence is necessary—his is conclusive.

TWO: You feel that animals understand things we do not?

ONE: As long as you are not referring to conceptual understanding, can you doubt it? If you do—that can only be because you have not yet understood, yourself.

TWO: Is it not just that we judge everything—including the "intelligence" of animals—from the point of view of conceptualisation, as though the formation of concepts comprised all forms of intelligence?

ONE: Undoubtedly, and when we begin to learn that conceptual thought is the supreme barrier to enlightenment, which is another word for All-knowledge, we begin to perceive the falsity of such a judgement.

TWO: Because conceptual thought, which is dualistic thought, based on a comparison of opposites, is *necessarily* erroneous? It is useful in phenomenal living, but is fundamentally false, and truth can only be known by by-passing it?

ONE: That readily becomes obvious as soon as one begins really to understand.

TWO: Then animals are not handicapped from the point of view of enlightenment?

ONE: I doubt if that term is correct for them, but since they lack the heavy handicap of human wickedness their path to *sagesse* should be relatively smooth.

TWO: I find it somewhat terrifying!

[1] *Ed. note:* Lakshmi was a cow who resided at Ramana Maharshi's ashram for many years.

ONE: You well may! Not because you do not treat animals sympathetically, but because you remember your own past attitude towards them. Comfort yourself with the thought that those of them who are sages will understand—not conceptually but really.

TWO: And yet I have heard you declare yourself to be a Christian?

ONE: It may be presumption, but such is my belief. I was so baptised, and I have never regretted it. Alas, I may not be a good one, but I do my best within my poor capacities.

TWO: Being a Buddhist does not invalidate your Christianity?

ONE: Evidently we are not talking of the dogmas of any of the Christian churches. Dogmas apart, and dogmas are inevitably false since permanence in a world of mutation makes nonsense, where is there incompatibility? Ramakrishna became in turn a Buddhist, a Christian, and a Muslim, and he had pictures of each Prophet on his walls to the end—yet he never ceased to be himself a Prophet of Vedanta Advaita. He recognised Truth wherever it was to be found.

TWO: And Buddhism, being more fully developed than any other religion, is large enough to include them all?

ONE: I will not dispute it, but I would rather say that Truth is one wherever it may be apprehended.

TWO: Will Christianity ever outgrow its dead dogma and reflower?

ONE: Where Truth is, Truth must prevail. Does its mask matter? Changing religion changes nothing but that which conceals the Truth.

TWO: Despite the human arrogance inculcated by the Christian churches you would have me remain a Christian?

ONE: If you can see the truth you can ignore the error. All conceptual life is error. You know it as void, the void of annihilation. It is not at all. There is plenty of that in the decadent forms of Buddhism, as in all the others.

TWO: If I did change my religion, what would you say?

ONE: Say? Why nothing, of course! I would just laugh!

40 ⁓ When the Dreamer Awakes

Dr. Suzuki gives us a perfect illustration of the Void. It is the Zen master's reply that the Buddha(-mind) is like a bucket of water with a hole in the bottom. When the water has drained out the bucket is *empty,* and *that* is the Void. That emptiness of concept is the Buddha-mind, or pure Consciousness, or Suchness.

Negation is the only way to purge the mind of all obstacles. It is the great cleanser.

Without total negation, negation of all dualistic perception and cognition, without absolute negation, the Void which is "Reality" cannot be realized—and that realization is Awakening.

Until every tie to the dream-world is broken, how could there be awakening?

When our dream-*sosie* knows himself to be *everything* in his dream-world what happens? The dreamer would find that he is no longer dreaming: inevitably he would be awake.

So it is in the living-dream: when any dreamed-*sosie* realizes that he is identical with everything in the living-dream, and that everything is identical with (is nothing but) him-self—he finds that he is awake, i.e. *that he is the dreamer also.* For dreamed, dreamer and dream are one, that is just dream-*ing.*

41 ᐧ Explanations, 1

To whole-mind *samsara* is perceived as *nirvana.*
To split-mind *nirvana* is perceived as *samsara.*
That is why they are identical.

But *nirvana* is noumenon, and *samsara* is phenomenon.
Both, however, as such, are concepts only and unreal.
The Buddha said it: they are identical, but neither exists.
Their reality can only be indicated by terms such as "Void" or "Emptiness."

Similarly, to whole-mind, Form (and each *skandha*) is per-ceived as Void,
To split-mind Void is perceived as Form (and each *skandha*).
That is why they are identical.

But Void, the unmanifested, is noumenon, and Form, the manifested, is phenomenon.
Both, again, as such, are just concepts, and neither exists.
Their reality can only be indicated by a term such as "Suchness" or "Isness."
And that reality can never be "relative."

Non-Duality

Unity can be found only in negation.

The resolution of any pair of opposites, which constitute two concepts, cannot be a third concept. It is a negative. It is neither, not both. It is a no-concept.

Therefore it cannot be conceived, and that is because it is "real" and concepts are not.

If you abstract the characteristics of both, that is the interpretation projected on to them by split-mind, that which is left is an absence, absence of own-being or of self-nature, which is the form of their Suchness.

Only I-am-not can see subject and object as one.

The reality of opposing concepts lies exclusively in no-mind itself. Only pseudo-subject sees them as two. Concepts no longer, they are pure subjectivity.

42 · Debunking the Relative

Nowhere in the sutras or in the recorded words of the Masters do we find the modern differentiation between "Reality" and the world of Appearance regarded as "Relative Reality," and distinguished by the use of the term "to be" for the one, and the verb "to exist" for the other. Moreover we are told categorically that *Nirvana* and *Samsara* are identical.

This way of understanding has seemed very helpful; in a sense it seems to explain almost everything. But does it? We cannot maintain that the Masters were not sufficiently intelligent to think of this device. I call it so here and now, for that is what I believe it to be. Nor can we maintain that they could not find a couple of words by means of which this differentiation could be conveyed. That they did not use it can only mean that it does not lead in the right direction, and that it would constitute a hindrance rather than a help—as we now imagine it to be. Moreover it is simply not true. There can be no such thing as a relative aspect of "Reality." And, if there could be, our apparent world is certainly not that. Finally, to seek to explain everything by this intellectual dualism does not seem likely to lead to that unity of vision which is what the Masters sought to enable us to obtain.

They spoke from their Buddha-nature, direct from whole-mind in whole-mind in so far as that could be done in the dualistic medium of words, and often they resorted to action instead. They only spoke of "Reality" and of that which is not "real" at all, for there are no half-measures of "reality," and there cannot be a semi-"reality" beside "Reality" itself. That may be an invention due to the I-concept subtly trying to maintain its foothold and keep us under its domination. If that be so, than let us call that bluff and demolish that stronghold! And if this device has indeed helped, is it not nevertheless a raft that must be left behind now that it has served its purpose?

This, indeed, was pointed out, briefly perhaps, in *Fingers Pointing Towards the Moon*. It is made abundantly clear in Han Shan's commentary on the Heart Sutra; it is true that he uses the term "relative reality," or his translator does, but in order to describe the void of annihilation—that which is not "real" at all. And, anyhow, how can *Samsara*, which is only an interpretation by split-mind, which is merely an event in the psyche, have relative reality? Finally, in "Explanations, 1," it becomes evident that there is no place for relativity in "reality." "Reality" is only a concept anyhow!

If there is no room for relative "reality" in the identity of *Nirvana* and *Samsara*, or in that of Void and *skandhas*, nor is there room for such a concept in the resolution of any pair of opposites. The resolution of subject and object, which is the direct way to awakening according to Huang Po, is not possible for split-mind to achieve. We cannot have two thoughts at once, and two consecutive concepts cannot be united by a third concept. Unity can only be found in the negative; never by a union of the two, but only in the negation of each. When the interpretation of split-mind is removed that which remains is the suchness for which we were looking in the opposite direction. Nothing relative can be therein.

The Masters spoke directly from Subjectivity, never (in these cases, such as the *prajna-paramita* doctrine) from pseudo-subject; always they spoke from whole-mind, and always of "reality." For them there was nothing but that, and they saw the phenomenal world via "reality" and not as anything apart. For them there was only the verb "to be," never the verb "to exist," though the latter is often used in translation as a substitute for "to be" because current language so uses it: never is it used in differentiation from it. It was necessary that their disciples should see in this manner, from a single point of view, from one only, never from two, from that of "reality," not from the "real" and the phenomenal alternatively. Obliging us to see from the point of view of "reality" only, and the phenomenal via (through) that, must surely be the only means whereby we may perceive the unity of the opposites, both concepts being dissolved in the negation of each.

How does this apply to us? Must we try to know that? We cannot know it. But we are not relatively "real," as we have been told that we are. As objects of pseudo-subject we have no "reality" whatever (we are the void of annihilation, if you wish). As pseudo-subject we have no "reality" whatever either—for pseudo-subject is not subject at all but just object. Both are conceptual objects of I-subject, the dreaming consciousness of our apparent living-dream. As concepts neither of these exist either (or is), but as no-subject and no-object, that is as nothing known to us, they are void. "Void of Reality" can be thought of as impersonal subjectivity, suchness, isness, and pure unconscious consciousness. Not very heartening? Not even very clear? Sorry, but we are speaking of "Reality"—and there are no concepts therein.

This seems a faint and far-off nebulosity? How badly I must have failed to portray us! We are that which is nearest and most present, and we fill every silence with our ubiquitous "reality." Perhaps I described our presence in terms of our absence? Or were you trying to catch sight of the dreamer without waking up?

By the way—and as Huang Po might have added, as in an afterthought—of course there is not "really" any such thing as "Reality" anyhow.

43 ⸗ The Gateway

Perhaps nothing more significant has ever been said than the simple statement of Hui Neng: "From the beginning not a thing is." Its greatness, strange to say, has always been recognised, and we all know it, for it has the simplicity of Truth.

But we forget that in that statement reality also is excluded from being, for it too is a "thing," a concept, and the word "real" can be added to the last word without affecting the meaning of the declaration.

Have we understood how important it is to realize that there is no such thing as reality in our universe, that reality is not, does not exist for us, for speaking of it as though it were something leads us astray and confirms us in error, plunging us deeper in the abyss of ignorance.

All there can be for us is non-reality, and the counterpart of that we *can not* know. Why? Obviously because there never was, is not, and never will be anything "outside" ourselves, any "thing" at all or any idea that could exist of itself, in its own right, which would be necessary in order that it should be real. Nothing objective can be. Even subject cannot be, for, in being recognised as subject, it thereby becomes an object.

Of course we can speak of Subjectivity, Absolute, Mind Only, pure Consciousness, as symbols, but then symbols are symbolical of something! In so far as they may be necessary for the communication of ideas we may use these words as indications, as pointers, and "reality" also, but we would do well not to forget that Huang Po, after a long dissertation on "Mind," ended his discourse by casually pointing out that of course there was not really any such *thing*. That surely was the culminating point, the essential, of his dissertation.

Let us follow his inestimable lead, here as always—for he was one of the greatest and clearest of awakened teachers; only Non-"reality" is, and it is the Gateway.

44 ~ Explanations, 2

Skandhas, seen as objects, are inexistent, i.e. are "the void of annihilation."

Skandhas, as subject of manifestation, are "the Void of Prajna," which is pure subjectivity,

And "The Void of Prajna," pure subjectivity, is each *skandha* as subject of manifestation.

But subject and object are not two things: They are the moon and the reflection of the moon. There are no objects, objects are not: They are just subjectivity looking at itself, i.e. dreaming.

45 ·~ Explanations, 3

Non-Reality

Everything we can know is a concept based on a percept, sensorial or imagined.

But no concept can be real, for by definition reality is immutable or that which is always identical with itself.

Reality, as such, however, is itself a concept and, therefore, unreal, devoid of reality.

It is evident that the Void of Reality should not mean the Void that is Reality, but that which is void *of* reality (devoid of the concept of reality).

So that a concept is void of reality, and void-of-reality is voidness of concept.

Non-reality only can be real.

Such being the situation as seen by split-mind (reasoning by comparison of opposites), that is why reality can only be non-reality—as far as we are concerned—so that they are identical.

Their identity lies in this—that if that which appears as reality to the divided aspect of mind *is* inevitably non-reality, to whole-mind that non-reality must necessarily be real.

46 ·~ Explanations, 4

Relative Reality

It will readily be seen that where there is no such thing as reality there can be nothing that is relative to reality, and so nothing that can be called "relative reality." It is indeed a nonsensical term, for the only thing that can be relative to nothing is nothing. No doubt we are that: only so-conceived can the expression have any sense.

As relative to a non-existent reality our phenomenal world cannot be anything at all and so-calling it, calling it relative, means that our eyes are looking in the wrong direction, and are holding us in bondage.

The only way out of bondage is by understanding that nothing is, no object whatever, not even ourselves as objects.

In that apparent void we may then be enabled to see ourselves and to perceive that what we are and our objective world could be, all we and our dream of living could possibly be, that which alone perhaps we are as awakened dreamers, is that so-called subjectivity, or noumenon, which is *non-manifestation* perceiving itself as manifested phenomena.

47 ᵕ Elimination

Attempting to perceive *Nirvana* from *Samsara* (via the *samsaric* mind) is surely absurd, for so seen *Nirvana* can only be a concept!

We must perceive *Samsara* from *Nirvana* (via whole-mind): they will then be seen as one, for they have only one suchness.

To seek anything non-*samsaric* via the *samsaric* mind must be absurd, for nothing can be seen from that direction: Huang Po said so many times ("you cannot reach Mind by means of mind, or the Buddha by means of the Buddha"). And that is surely why the Masters nearly always spoke from whole-mind and left their disciples to understand what they could!

So let us stop talking about it, thinking about it, and start doing! Neither by talking nor by thinking can it be done.

That was why the T'ang Masters acted rather than talked. Whole-mind is always with us, and only ourself hides it from us. If we leave ourself behind—we are it.

Ourself is only a mask—a *persona*—and can be dropped like a cloak. Ramakrishna spoke of doing that, as did Jesus in an apocryphal saying that has an air of authenticity. Both no doubt have been taken literally, physically, and why not? The physical act is a symbol of the metaphysical, and for either or for both the same psychic adjustment is needed. Nakedness, on whatever plane, requires of the artificially conditioned an abandonment of the consciousness of self, which alone is what matters. Nudity and transparence imply the same condition—the freeing of body and mind of all that does not appertain to their own nature. If the sage is said to be transparent that is because the Buddha-nature is not opaque, and that alone remains.

The Buddha-nature, sometimes called our "original nature," seen by us is again a negative; it is just Not-self (that which is not self, or that which remains when self is eliminated).

Similarly, that which remains when self is eliminated, that is Non-reality, is what we seek to imagine as Suchness.

48 ⊷ The Essential Understanding

The essential understanding surely is just this: as that which we think we are, we are nothing, we *are* not. But as Nothing (nothing we can know as anything), as that which "we" are not, we are everything that is or could ever be. Not, of course, of course, as individuals, "individuals," as objects—which we never were and never could be—but as that Nothing which is not. Not, of course, of course, as human beings—which are figments only—but as the unmanifested which is the subject of manifestation.

Becoming a Bamboo

I don't think that can be expressed as a syllogism, but it can be apprehended intuitionally, and it can be indicated by means of verbal manipulation, capital letters, inverted commas etc., as above.

If we differentiate further we are separating *Nirvana* and *Samsara*, and they have to be seen as one. There are *not* two points of view—ours and the "real": that is an explanation that is not valid because it is looking in the wrong direction. There is only one way of looking that is valid, and it cannot be syllogistically expressed precisely because it is two opposing points of view perceived as one. There is, however, no point of view that is "ours" and there is nothing that is "real": both must be seen negatively—for "our" point of view is a figment, and "reality" is non-reality to us. It is from a realization of this essential *non*-reality that it is possible to apprehend what we are, and that that is everything we can know. One Master advocated "becoming a bamboo." That, properly understood, should give us the necessary apprehension.

Let us try again, in another locution: That which (*samsarically*) we think we are, that (*nirvanically*) we are not. But as that (*samsarically* conceived) nothing "we" (which we are not) are everything that seems to be. For that (*samsarically* conceived) nothing is (*nirvanically*) the inconceivable and so unnameable, which we can indicate only by some term, which *must be* negative, such as "Void" or "Non-manifestation."

But, withal, *Samsara*, *nirvanically* perceived, is not other than that *nirvanic* perception.

49 ⁓ *The Shrine of Subjectivity*

If one abides in subjectivity one is no longer an object.

Others think they see one as such, but that which they see is not us but their object.

One is not sensorially perceptible when one is in a state of subjectivity—since one is not an object and the apparent object is not us.

One is invulnerable and unattainable in that mode, for one is not, and one's only manifestation is benediction.

That is why the sages do not appear to react; it is also the reason why their apparent actions are the expression of non-action.

This state is accessible to us as it is to them: it is the common heritage of us all because it is all that we are.

In order to enjoy it we have only to withdraw into our *bodhimandala*.

Note: A *bodhimandala* is a little shrine to which one retires in order to place oneself in a state of availability for enlightenment; but the term is essentially metaphorical.

Vista

"This consciousness exists as each being, and nothing else exists."

(Centering, N.99 from the Vigyan Bhairava and Sochanda Tantra.)

Yes, indeed! Nothing else exists or is, was, will be, or ever could be.

Consciousness is all that is—and it is not anything, neither thing nor concept, nor even nothing.

It is neither Void nor Plenum, empty nor full, neither being nor non-being. It has neither form nor name nor the absence of anything.

It is that which remains when we become aware that there could never be anything whatsoever, least of all ourselves.

It is the ocean in which we are eddies.

50 ·- Colloquially, 1

"Neither" not "Both": The Reason Why

When we think of "love" or "hate," or feel them, of "liking" or "disliking," of something being "good" or not so "good," all these are just egocentric interpretations of a percept. They are evaluations, judgements: none of them is in itself any sort or kind of a "thing."

How, then, could anyone hope to conceive two contradictory evaluations as one—since there is nothing present except two mental estimations perceived separately?

In order to see "both" as one it would be necessary to have two contradictory thoughts combined into one thought—which is not possible.

It is clear that these are not anything external that can be perceived as such, but that they are subjective interpretations only.

When we have realized this, we can see them as nothing, i.e. that neither is anything at all. Then, and only then, perhaps, does it become possible to find the way towards this essential understanding which we know opens the mind to awakening.

So let us enquire what it is that is interpreted, evaluated, estimated as one or other of these, and other, subjective judgements. Evidently that which is so judged is a perception, sensorial or imagined, physical or psychic, and do we not know that a pure (uninterpreted) perception appertains to our "original nature" which it was the constant aim of the Masters to reveal to us via our own apprehension (never by just "telling" us and so giving us an intellectual interpretation of it)?

Surely it must be that "pure" perception which is the resolution, the unification, of any two elements of a pair of opposites, and, surely, nothing else whatever could be that? Was it not to that end that the Masters posed a problem and cried "Speak! Speak!" before their disciples had time to start thinking? Was that not the reason for all their strange answers, as for all their rough gestures which obviated the use of words—since words are for us the expression of thoughts?

Perhaps we have only to look in the right direction in order to perceive the answer—with spontaneity, so that the mechanism of thoughts, dominated by the notion of "I," may be eliminated?

51 ·~ Colloquially, 2

The Skandhas

Does not this also explain the apparent mystery of the famous *skandhas*, which are declared on the one hand to be nothing, the void of annihilation, and, on the other, the Void of Prajna?

As concepts it is evident that they are nothing, for then they are objects only, or interpretations, but as "pure" percepts they may be our "original nature"?

"Form" is physical—since we like to differentiate everything—that is perceiving the physical: the other four are psychic—that is perceiving the imagined. Their differentiation into four concepts expressed in four terms is almost impossible for us to use, since the qualified philologists give us half-a-dozen different words for each, to choose from. But together they describe our apprehensive faculties in their dynamic aspect, and as such, I think, they represent "pure" subjectivity, without any interference from the pseudo-subject. Each seems to be an element of all that sentient beings can be said to be as manifestations of the unmanifested.

Therefore must they not indicate the "pure" perceiving of which we have just been speaking, that is the mechanism of that "pure" perceiving; not, of course, the psycho-somatic mechanism, but the transitional "mechanism," if it may be so called, or rather the "mechanism" of manifestation itself. They may be likened to the prismatic elements by means of which pure light is transformed into the appearance of many colours.

As objects, functions, concepts—they are nothing: as subjective "organs" of manifestation, but not, on any account, of interpretation, they may be the so-called Void of Prajna which, surely, is just subjectivity as such?

52 ⸺ Sidelights on Some Ko-ans, 1

Kakuan, a Master of the twelfth century, made a significant statement when he said: "Through delusion one makes everything (everything becomes) untrue. Delusion is not caused by objectivity; it is the result of (personal) subjectivity."

This seems to mean that everything interpreted by the mind that is subjected to an I-concept is delusion, but that if that false identification is eliminated perceptions (then "pure" perceptions) are not delusive, for they are purely objective.

We can now understand what the T'ang Masters meant when they held up a *hossu,* a stick, a pot or other object, and cried, "Do not say it is a *hossu,* a stick, a pot or other object; do not say it is not; what is it? Speak! Speak!" The poor, mystified monks were nonplussed, for the Masters never explained anything, knowing that it was essential that the understanding should come from within and not from without.

But we have to understand, for we have no Masters, and they meant that if the object were given its name that would be an interpretation by split-mind, a concept, delusory and unreal; what they sought to arouse was just a pure perception of the object, uninterpreted, which either should produce awakening or open the way for it on a subsequent occasion.

That also, no doubt, is the explanation of the Flower Sermon of the Buddha, when only Mahakasyapa understood the silent holding-up of a flower—and he smiled, for he was awake.

That Masters strove to open the way for the "original nature" by short-circuiting the dualistic reasoning of identified mind.

53 ∙∽ *Sidelights on Some Ko-ans, 2*

Mu-mon in his collection of *ko-ans* called The Gateless Gate (No. 23) recounts the story of Hui Neng, pursued by E-myo who, failing to retrieve the Robe and the Bowl, asked for the Doctrine instead, and was immediately enlightened. The doctrine he was given was, "When you do not think good and when you do not think not-good, what is your true self (original nature)?"

Whatever we may think of this form of words as English, it gives the sense, whereas "good" and "evil," being abstract principles, set the mind looking in the wrong direction. What E-myo immediately apprehended was that everything he saw as pleasant or unpleasant, desirable or undesirable, better or worse, was a judgement dictated by an I-concept, and that he had been doing that, and nothing but that, from morning to night, all his life, as we all do. He also perceived that if he could really cease to do that even for a moment in which he would normally be doing it, for that moment the I-concept would be eliminated, and that what remained would be his "true self"—which has been better indicated by a term such as "original mind," "original face," or "Buddha nature."

Hui Neng, in one short phrase, revealed the whole problem, which is "the Doctrine," and opened the mind of his persecutor to the understanding he had vainly sought for so many years under the Fifth Patriarch.

54 ⁓ Sidelights on Some Ko-ans, 3

In another *ko-an* (No. 25) Mu-mon quotes Kyozan as declaring, "The truth of Mahayana teaching is transcendent, above words and thought. Do you understand?"

Mu-mon comments: "When he opens his mouth he is lost. When he seals his mouth he is lost. If he does not open it, if does not seal it, he is 108,000 miles from truth."

This is another example of what has just been set forth in No. 1 of these four Notes: if the pilgrim starts to interpret, evaluate, conceptualise, he is thereby and immediately "108,000 miles" in error.

He adds, in his habitual little poem:
> "In the light of day,
> Yet in a dream,
> He talks of a dream."

Yes, he too tells us that life in the light of day is a dream, and that nevertheless in that dream Man talks of a concept (necessarily if he talks)—which is another degree of dreaming. I have tried to explain elsewhere that this is more than just an image; it is an accurate description of what our life in fact is—in so far as it can be said to "be" at all.

We are reminded, on the one hand, of the Maharshi who tells us that if in the process of awakening from sleep we can hold our "identity" we shall indeed be awake, and forever, and, on the other hand, of the very ancient Vigyan Bhairava and Sochinda Tantra which say: "At the point of sleep when sleep has not yet come and external wakefulness vanishes, at this point *being* is revealed." (No. 50)

I have suggested elsewhere in this book that if, in either degree of dreaming, the identified subject were to realize that he himself was only an integral part of the dream-world in which he appears to figure, and was in no way different from, and certainly not "superior" to, or more "real" than, any other part he would inevitably awaken and know himself as the dreaming consciousness. This, too, seeks to express the same underlying intuition—the elimination of the servitude imposed by the I-notion, resulting in immediate apprehension of what the Chinese termed "the original nature."

55 ∙~ Sidelights on Some Ko-ans, 4

That same amusing Mu-mon, commenting on Joshu's answer—to the ritual query as to why the Bodhidarma came to China—"An oak-tree in the garden," almost as ritual as the query, says:

"Words cannot describe everything.

The heart's message cannot be delivered in words,

If one receives words literally, he will be lost,
If he tries to explain with words, he will not attain enlightenment in this life."

The fingers of the Master, of both Masters, Joshu and Mu-mon, point in the same direction as in the other ko-ans cited; words are not only valueless, as conveying concepts they constitute a barrier. A pure perception, be it what we know as an oak tree in any garden, a fig tree or a post in a courtyard, or any other object, on the other hand comes direct from the original nature or whole-mind. So important is this that Mu-mon declares that: "If one sees Joshu's answer clearly, there is no Shakyamuni Buddha before him and no future Buddha after him."

The inefficacy of words is evident indeed, and did not another Master say to his disciple who was worrying over a sutra, "Do not let yourself be put out by the sutra, put out the sutra instead!" That may have been all very well at that period in China, when there were several enlightened Masters in the province, but we have none to tell us when we are on the wrong path. Before we dare make free with the sutras we must find out what they mean, and what the Masters meant when they condescended to speak. We have to use words, fully realizing their limitations, before being in a position to discard them. Then indeed they must be abandoned.

56 ·- Void as the Non-Apparent Universe

Separated subject sees the world around him as *samsara*. Non-separated subject (subjectivity) sees that also, since it is "his" object, for separated subject sees at all because it is non-separated subject that is seeing, and "he" sees via the apparatus that separated subject regards as himself.

Such is *samsara*—and it is an objectivisation of subjectivity. When subjectivity does not objectivise, or, intemporally, where there is no objectivisation, there is no subject and there is only void, and that, being potential objectivisation, or objectivisation that is not seen as such, is the same as *samsara* so-called when seen via separated subject.

That no doubt is why potential objectivisation, void or *nirvana*, is said to be identical with *samsara*.

When subjectivity is not "looking," i.e. when objects are not perceived, that is non-manifestation, and not-looking or non-manifestation is *nirvana* or the "void."

But the "looking" of subjectivity, i.e. manifestation, is the objective functioning of sentient beings via their psychic apparatus. When a sentient being ceases to be a vehicle for subjectivity, that by means of which he has been sentient automatically becomes void, and when he functions as a vehicle for subjectivity the apparent universe immediately takes the place of the void which is the non-apparent universe.

Separated subject, of course, is not at all except as a vehicle for subjectivity, and he is void when he is not manifesting as a *skandha*; i.e. as part of the apparent universe, he is not. He is not anything but an object in the dream of manifestation in which he *plays the part* of subject.

Han Shan[1] points out that the Buddha's real meaning in the Heart Sutra is that *Prajna-Wisdom is the subject*, and the *skandhas* are the object thereof. "Prajna-Wisdom" and the "Void of Prajna" are two images which seek to indicate the indescribable, and that is the subject of all objects.

---

[1] *Ed. note:* Han-Shan was a 7th Century Chinese sage famous for his collection of poems and aphorisms entitled *Cold Mountain*.

Those sentient beings whose subjective element has disidentified itself with the role of separated subjects thereby "plunge" into the void, that is they find they are no longer objects playing the part of subjects. That which then remains is all that ever was, which is the subjectivity they represent. But that, when it has no object, is no longer subject, but just that voidness which is subjectivity that is not "looking," i.e. whose objects are not perceived. Being void, however, they are also subjectivity wherever there is objectivisation.

As subject they are the so-called "Void of Prajna": as objects they are the so-called "void of annihilation" for they have never existed.

57 ⸺ The Key of the Gateless Gate: The End of the Negative Way

The Void is not of the nature of a black abyss or a bottomless pit.

Rather is its nature "vast and expansive like space itself."

It is apprehended as "serene, marvellous, all-pure, brilliant and all-inclusive."

Above all does it partake of the nature of light.

And it is not anything.

For Void is Mind Itself, and Mind Itself is Void.

That is the answer.

Note: A key can only be used when the gate is reached. In order to reach the gate it is necessary to tread this long path through the jungle of conceptualised intuition.

58 · Hoorah!

Yes, you are right. This is where we come in, and all our friends—the donkeys, the lions, the beetles, the lilies-of-the-field and the cabbages-of-the-garden.

This is where we have always been in—for we are the subjectivity of Mind and imagine our*selves* to be its objects. If it is what we are, it is also what we are not, for it is void and there is no we therein.

And it is because it is void, because there is no we, that subjectivity is possible.

It is because we are not, that we appear to be.

Like everything else in the apparent universe.

59 · Débris, 2

What we mean by "mind" is probably just the conditioned aspect of consciousness.

But all that can be perceived (as an apperception) is Consciousness itself.

❧

The "objective realm" does not exist. It is a dream of subjectivity.

Duration, activity, passivity, belong exclusively to that.

Pure Consciousness is the non-being of deep sleep.

❧

The reason why *satori, wu, nirvana,* the Buddha-mind, the awakened state, has always been ours is that it is necessarily subjective—it is nothing but that which we are when "we" are not, i.e. pure consciousness.

As Tsung Kao[1] told us: "If you want to grasp it, it runs away from you, but if you cast it away it continues to be there all the time." Why? Because you would be making it an object and it is yourself—which you cannot "see."

※

Most of our difficulties, what the Masters describe as our "ignorance," result from our obsession with objects, from our congenital objectivisation of everything.

The answer, of course, is within, the subjective vision—Jesus Himself is recorded as having said it a couple of times at least.

[1] *Ed. note:* Ta-hui Tsung Kao (1089—1163), a Master of the Lin-Chi (Rinzai) school of Chan Buddhism.

PART III

Absolute Absence

❧

Presence with absolute absence,
Absence with absolute presence,
Presence with absence of being,
That is Absolute Absence.

—SHEN HUI

60 · Testamentary

TWO: If on your death-bed someone were to ask you what seemed to you to be the ultimate truth—what would you reply?

ONE: First of all I would say that none of us succeeds because we all stop half way, none of us ever goes right to the end of the road.

The ultimate teaching of the Buddha—the *Prajnaparamita*—tells us quite definitely if not clearly what is required of us. Either this message cannot be or should not be imparted simply and directly.

This teaching seems to be that no kind of reality exists or could exist, that it is only an idea and that it constitutes an impassable barrier around us. In whichever direction we look, no matter what theories we elaborate, we manufacture a "reality" and place it at the end of our field of vision. But there is not such a thing. And as long as we see like that we are looking in the wrong direction, and we will never see anything but a reflection of ourselves.

It does not in any way suffice to substitute non-reality for reality—because non-reality is a mode of reality. Both are inexistent.

Nor does it suffice to tell oneself that though neither the one nor the other exists for us in our dualistic servitude, nevertheless, behind the curtain of dualism, there lies reality. That is the ubiquitous pitfall. For *Nirvana* does not differ from *Samsara*—the sutras tell us that continually—and there is no reality outside manifestation either. In fact it is a will-o'-the-wisp which we must recognise as such: reality can never be anything but an idea, a notion, a concept of split-mind.

This is fundamental: as long as we see something "positive" at the end of our field of vision we shall not be able to find the way out of dualism; or something "negative" either, because both are aspects of one divided perception. The figure which represents us in our sleeping dreams cannot see the phenomenal reality that we see in our living-dream any more than we can see reality outside our dream, and neither, by awakening, would ever see a reality that was anything but phenomenal.

It has been said that reality is that which is immutable, or is that of whose existence it is not possible to doubt. These fine dualistic definitions are ropes with which we tie ourselves up and which hold us in bondage. Nothing is immutable, no thing whatever, and we should doubt everything, precisely because, as Hui Neng told us, nothing exists and nothing is. For no thing is at all, at all. I said NO THING (not a thing called "nothing," but no thing and no concept).

With this understanding we should be able at last to set forth, because, at last, we should have found the gateless gate.

Beyond, we should not expect to find ourselves in a world that is "positive," nor in a world that is "negative." For "we" should not BE either, because nothing is, not even us. The idea of being, also, is only an idea, a concept. We *are* only in dualistic manifestation—and that is a dream. Therefore it would not be possible for us to say what we are, because we would

ot be. No doubt that is why even the Buddha was not
ble to say it.

Not being, we should not need reality, which is
thereby revealed as a need exclusively belonging to the
dualistic state, that is to say a need that is imagined, like
the rest. Reality becomes superfluous, an anachronism,
a life-boat on land, or the raft that we leave behind
when it cannot carry us any further.

That is the ultimate message of the Buddha, as I
understand it, in the *Prajnaparamita* sutras. That is
going right to the end of the road. That which lies
beyond the gateway that awaits us there, no doubt
the only gateway in the iron curtain that surrounds
us, we can never know, not so much because we suppose that there is nothing there as because there is
nobody to know if there is anything there or not—
which comes to the same thing, since, without "anybody" there could not be any "thing."

How many times has not the Buddha told us that
there is neither entity nor *dharma*, neither person nor
thing? Are we surprised to find by ourselves that he
spoke the truth, that everything he said holds good?
And what could be simpler or clearer?

Is not this the key which opens the gate which is
not one, and which, so-doing, dissipates all the mysteries and apparent contradictions in the sutras and
in the superficially obscure sayings of the Masters?

TWO: Why should we not speak of that which lies beyond
conceptual knowledge as "reality"?

ONE: Because by thinking of something as real or as
unreal there is necessarily a subject that observes an

object, and as long as that process continues we are still tied to the world of phenomena.

In pure negation there is no object, and without an object there can be no subject: one is no longer. It is just that which we have to understand—*that we are not.*

Once that is understood, perhaps then it will be possible once more to see mountains as mountains and rivers as rivers, but in a perspective that was not available before.

How is that? At the limit of our present comprehension there seems to be pure consciousness, called the One-Mind or No-Mind in Buddhism, and the Self or Atma in Vedanta. As we have seen, this is void—"the" Void if you must make an entity of it. But this "empty" consciousness manifests, and this manifestation is the objectivisation of subjectivity which consciousness inevitably is.

We, objects believing ourselves to be subjects, perceive this manifestation, which is our universe, of which we are, because each of the elements called *skandhas,* which, as we know, are identical with subjectivity-void, "uses" the object which is the psycho-somatic apparatus which we regard as ours, if not as ourselves, in order to project the manifest universe.

On the path to enlightenment we perceive: (1) the world—referred to as "mountains and rivers"—as real; (2) later, we perceive them as illusory objects of consciousness, and so, unreal; and (3) when we are awakened, we know them as consciousness itself, manifesting as "mountains and rivers," that is to say as heretofore but with this difference of perspective.

But this third perception is not a perception of reality: it is still phenomenal, a conceptualised perception.

But knowing ourselves as this still conceptual pure consciousness is already to know ourselves as void—because it is void; it is nevertheless to know ourselves as not being anything that is "positive," "real," or "personal."

There could not be any "we" in pure consciousness that is void. Pure consciousness is not anything but a way of indicating that into which all ideas of separate selfdom must necessarily dissolve. It is the solvent, the catalyser of our conceptual notion of being—for once "we" know ourselves to be that, "we" are not any longer.

61 ·- A Pink Elephant?

How could reality possibly be known? As long as "we" still exist as individuals how could we know reality—since that would just be a concept?

And if "we" were no longer, as such, who would there be to know anything whatsoever!

If, indeed, there were such a thing as reality, it could never be possible to find out what it was. Therefore the notion of its existence seems to be perfectly gratuitous. At best it is a piece of laboratory apparatus—and imaginary at that!

62 ⸱⁓ No-Mind, No-Mirror

If life indeed has a spiral pattern one might suppose that Western "Zen" is now swinging round over the period of Shen Hsiu and Hui Neng.

Bodhidharma brought to China the teaching of the Negative Way, but by the time of the fifth Patriarch it had become the property of a small sect which had developed it into a positive doctrine looking for reality somewhere inside its own head, instead of outside like the rest of mankind.

When the fifth Patriarch felt the need of a successor he asked for an epitome of the doctrine, and Shen Hsiu, the leading member of the sect, wrote his famous lines, stating that the body is like the Bodhi Tree, the mind like a bright mirror, and that we must keep that mirror clean and allow no dust to settle on it. That is typical positive doctrine; the mind—we may find the word "consciousness" happier—is again being likened to a mirror, a vast, imperishable reflector whose purity must be maintained, for it represents reality. No doubt the image is a good one, no doubt mind is well represented thus, but so seeing it just gets us nowhere, as it got no one anywhere under the fifth Patriarch.

The fifth Patriarch knew the truth, but he does not seem to have been able or willing to propound it. He also knew that Hui Neng knew it, and only Hui Neng, whose unconditioned mind realized it while listening to the Diamond Sutra, but he felt unable to impose that young peasant, illiterate at that, on his learned sect as his successor. So he gave Hui Neng the opportunity of making public what he knew. And Hui Neng got someone to write up for him the same number of lines, stating that there never was a Bodhi Tree, that there was no bright mirror, that from the beginning nothing whatever existed, and that there was nowhere for dust to alight.

This was not well received, but the facts had been publicly stated, and the fifth Patriarch could give Hui Neng the robe and the bowl, but he had to smuggle him out of the monastery, and it was fifteen years before Hui Neng, sixth Patriarch by right of the robe and the bowl, was publicly recognised.[1] From that moment the doctrine spread like wild-fire, and within a generation or two it attained its fullest development and its widest appeal.

Today the West has its Shen Hsius, and the little sect is busy polishing its mirrors, keeping the dust off them, and searching for reality therein—pardon, for Reality. But it is Hui Nengs that are needed again.

Indeed the teaching of Hui Neng has not been forgotten (the spiral pattern works like that)—perhaps the teaching of Bodhidharma was not forgotten in the days of the fifth Patriarch. It was just conveniently ignored—as it is being today. And just as the little sect led by Shen Hsiu, learned and very worthy man as he almost certainly was, continued to ignore the teaching, so the modern I-church will no doubt do likewise. I do not so call it in scorn, for it is a noble doctrine. Moreover—at least in my small opinion—it is a true doctrine, but it is not the direct path brought to China by Bodhidharma, not the direct path taught by Hui Neng: it is not the path of the great *prajnaparamita* sutras which alone are that. It is a long path indeed, because the I-concept too is a pilgrim, a pilgrim who leads the others astray at every turning, and who is only pushed over the precipice at the very

---

[1] He was not finally recognised as Sixth Patriarch until 75 years after his death, and as a result of Shen Hui's life-long proclamation of his doctrine.

end. The direct path is the Negative Way, along which no I-concept can travel—for a shadow cannot travel by itself.

63 ·~ *Cracking the Nut*

TWO: Be a good chap and give me a ko-an. Don't raise your eyebrows, just give it.

ONE: Who?

TWO: You mean *Wu?*

ONE: It might do, but I prefer the English spelling, without an "h."

TWO: I don't know it as a ko-an.

ONE: Nonsense. The Maharshi gave it to everyone who pestered him—in the form of "Who Am I?"

TWO: He was not a Zen Buddhist.

ONE: Are any of us? Perhaps the grand old man of Chan, Hsu Yun, heir of the Patriarchs, who died recently aged 119, was a good enough Zen Buddhist? If not, I don't know of a better since Huang Po. His was "Who is the one who recites the name of the Buddha?" But "Who?" is the point.

TWO: That is a well-known Chan *hua-t'ou.*

ONE: Nationalism in such matters is ridiculous. The technique of using these formula may differ, but their aim is identical—direct seeing by cutting out thought.

TWO: Very well, but what is the answer?

ONE: It is for you to give me that.

TWO: To me the answer could only be "subjectivity," but I give it from knowledge, not from direct seeing.

ONE: What a pernickety fellow you are! When you know it you can no longer give it as a result of direct seeing—unless by re-seeing.

TWO: But I know it as a result of years of consideration of the problem.

ONE: No doubt, but you have seen it nevertheless. We in the West have no Masters to subject us to the exigencies of these oriental techniques: we have to find out as best we may—by understanding. Provided we have really seen it, that is enough: reasoning may open the way to direct seeing.

TWO: Very well. But what is subjectivity?

ONE: Look, and tell me what you see.

TWO: What I see is void.

ONE: Of course. And why?

TWO: In looking I behold an object, I have to, and that is all I see.

ONE: Inevitably. And the reason for that?

TWO: I know of no reason for anything so unreasonable.

ONE: Come, come! Who is looking?

TWO: I am, of course.

ONE: And who is "I"?

TWO: I have just told you—subjectivity.

ONE: Quite so. And can an eye see itself?

TWO: No, it cannot.

ONE: So what does it see when it tries to turn itself into an object?

TWO: Nothing.

ONE: Exactly.

TWO: You mean that that is why so-called void is such?

ONE: But of course! An eye cannot see itself, neither can an "I."

Absolute Absence

TWO: But... but... all these definitions of the famous "Void"....

ONE: Definitions are always of an object. You have seen that in Han Shan's demonstration of the Heart Sutra the "Void" is called "the Void of Prajna," also that it was the intention of the Buddha to make it clear that Prajna was the Subject. It follows that the "Void" is "Subject" and that "Subject" is the "Void." When looked at, of course, and—since there is no-one else to look—looked at by itself. Elementary.

TWO: Elementary, my foot, or perhaps to you when you have seen it, but who knows it, who has said it?

ONE: I have no idea, but anyone can presumably see the obvious.

TWO: But Nirvana and all that. Are they that too?

ONE: I cannot answer for "all that," but for Nirvana—of course. I dare say as much nonsense has been written about the so-called "Void" as about anything else.

TWO: Let me readjust my ideas! For years we have been cudgelling our brains about the "Void" and what it could and could not be, and all the time it is only what subjectivity cannot see because it cannot see itself?

ONE: Subjectivity cannot be its own object. There is no other void, apart from a word that indicates "nothing" and that may be applied in any context—the void of annihilation, as Han Shan calls it. That last is only the verbal counterpart of "something."

TWO: Then Samsara, which is said to be identical with Nirvana?

ONE: Samsara is subjectivity seeing—the objectivising of subjectivity or subjectivity functioning. Since there is nothing else, nothing but subjectivity, how could they not be identical?

TWO: Objectivity, samsara, is just I, every I, every eye of subjectivity objectivising and thereby projecting objects whenever it does so, which is whenever I, every I, every eye, looks?

ONE: You put things in your own language, but clearly, on the rare occasions on which you see something.

TWO: Thanks, old man. But I am not through yet. Everything is that, even the body, perceptions, feelings, thoughts, consciousness?

ONE: You have just described the *skandhas*, except that as you have put it they have to be regarded as objects. In fact their function is dynamic, for they are the psychic mechanisms of samsara, so that they should rather be described as body-consciousness, perceptivity, sensitivity, mentation, and conditioned consciousness. Otherwise they would be *dharmas* only, which, of course they are as objects, whereas it is their subjective function which renders them identical with "the Void" or pure subjectivity regarded as an object.

TWO: But surely samsara too is composed of *dharmas?*

ONE: Samsara too when regarded just as objects; as identical with the "Void" samsara would be more clearly described as "perceiving samsara," "the" perceiving if you wish, for the objects as such are not anything.

TWO: So that is why there is only a "seeing," and no see-er nor any-"thing" seen. Subjectivity is the key. Is there anything to prevent one from sorting out the whole ghastly muddle?

ONE: The whole ghastly muddle is only due to looking for objects. When you look subjectively, there is no muddle at all—unless you contrive to think another one up.

TWO: One puzzle remains.

ONE: I doubt it.

TWO: The most vital problem of all.

ONE: Out with it: you make me quite nervous!

TWO: The identity of subject and object, whose reunion is all that we need?

ONE: Subjectivity is subject, of course, and its objectivisation is object, of course.

TWO: And they are one?

ONE: The objectivising of subjectivity is utterly itself—for there is nothing but itself: it is that and that is it, and when it looks at itself via *skandhas* it sees Nothing, which is Voidness. In Voidness, in Nothing, which is what it then sees, subject and object are one.

TWO: And when I, as subjectivity, which is all I am, see subjectivity as void, I see subject and object as one?

ONE: You then *apprehend yourself* as void, in which subject and object are necessarily one. And that is why you wake up—for you are no longer an *object*. But you must apprehend that, and not just think it.

TWO: Which is *paravritti*, the turning over of the mind, the further dimension of vision which we seek?

ONE: It is the vision whereby an I sees itself as No-I and therefore *is* I.

TWO: What then is subjectivity when it is not projecting the apparent universe via its own projected *skandha* mechanisms?

ONE: It is known to us as "pure consciousness"—pure implying consciousness unconditioned by the projected universe of duality; it is subjectively quiescent. And that, too, is void, the same, the only void, because void, not "a" or "the" void. For it also is consciousness subjectively regarded (by itself subjectively) as an object, and as such it is just experienced as bliss and universal benediction.

64 ·~ This World of "Ours"

Samsara is a subjective state.

It is a see-ing whereby subjectivity projects apparent objects by means of apparent subjects.

This is called Duality.

These apparent subjects, negative as are all subjects, project apparent objects, positive as are all objects, via a psychic mechanism known as *skandhas* whenever their subjectivity becomes identified with a supposed aggregation of such *skandhas*.

The apparent subjects and objects, as objects, are in no way different but, the subjects being negative and the objects positive, when they are perceived in the same direction of measurement, or dimension, or are "superimposed," mutually fulfil one another (as do a photographic negative and positive), and then present a blank uniformity. So regarded they are no longer apparent as subject and object: they are one and void.

Nirvana is also a subjective state.

It is a no-seeing whereby subjectivity, since it cannot perceive itself, is not manifest.

This is called Non-duality.

Both states, which as subjectivity are identical, can only be differentiated by the projections known as sentient beings, whose faculty of apprehension is itself subjectivity, via the *skandha*-mechanism, and whose objective appearance is a projection of subjectivity as *Samsara*.

Consequently, by a union or "superimposition" of the two states, negative and positive, they mutually fulfil one another and become a blank uniformity or void, which is represented by the term "pure consciousness."

This is the resolution of false dualities such as Non-duality and Duality, of *Nirvana* and *Samsara*, of subject and object, and it is always void.

Note: There is no objective state, and there "are" no objects. Consciousness, experienced as subjectivity, alone "is," and it is NOT.

65 ·- *Neti Neti*

Samsara is not things, but a seeing of things.

This seeing is the positive counterpart of the negative which is *Nirvana*.

Therefore Nirvana is also not any thing, but is a negative seeing or a seeing of no-things (a seeing that is a no-seeing, as Dr. Suzuki has put it).

There are no things in either—any more than there are in photographs, but light and shade only, distributed negatively as in *Nirvana*, then positively, when reversed, as in *Samsara*. The photographic film, however, is a projected object, whereas *Nirvana* is the subjective vision of the apparatus itself.

Where a positive photograph shows a dark tree against a pale sky, the negative shows a pale tree-shaped hole in a dark background. The tree is a product of the imagination, an interpretation projected on to a pattern of light and shade.

The tree photographed is a positive apparent object in *Samsara* (of samsaric seeing) whose negative is no-tree, likewise a hole in a background, and that is in *Nirvana* (of nirvanic seeing). Both are phenomenal, but it is from no-tree that apparent-tree is deduced via its positive.

Manifestation is always positive, and it is always the reversal of the negative, which is non-manifestation. The interpretation, being phenomenal, creates the image which thereby becomes an object.

When nirvanic seeing and samsaric seeing are combined in unified vision, just as when a positive and a negative film are superimposed, the resulting object is nil. It is blank, void, for the light and shade of each has been compensated by the other, so that there is no variation anywhere that can be interpreted as a thing, that is as an object; and that is why *Nirvana* and *Samsara* are necessarily identical. Since there is nothing that can be interpreted, nothing that can be described, that is the void or voidness.

Voidness is split into negative and positive, *Nirvana* and *Samsara*, whenever subjectivity is reflected in objects which thereby mistake themselves for subjects seeing objects that are interpreted as real.

No object is real. No object exists. Every object, physical or psychic, is an interpretation only.

Subjectivity alone is, and its nirvanic vision via the *skandhas* is the negative aspect of suchness, its positive vision, a subsequent reversal of that, in time, via the senses, is the samsaric, and the apparent universe of our living dream is a perceptive and conceptual interpretation of that objectivisation of suchness via the positive of a negative sensorial apperception.

Absolute Absence

Nirvana and *Samsara* are not true dualities. Nor are
ject and object, non-being and being, non-reality and reality,
non-duality itself and duality. They are "appréciations con-
trastantes," alternative aspects or ways of looking. They are a
confrontation of subjectivity with itself. Therefore they are
identical, and their identity needs no demonstration. Non-
manifestation likewise is the negative and the subject, which
is at the same time manifestation, its positive and its apparent object. In the same line of vision, or "superimposed," that
is seen "vertically," they become void and the principal of
suchness or potentiality.

There is no more to be said, for ultimately that is every-
thing that is—as far as we can ever know—and that is *Neti
Neti*, *Wu Wu*, not this not that, not any thing whatsoever.
Which would seem to be the pure doctrine of the
Prajnaparamita which Shen Hui declares to be absolutely
essential to comprehension.

Note: Hui Neng instructed his successors to use contraries in all
replies to questions, so as to induce an understanding of their identity. When subjectivity is understood there are not any dualities any
longer.

66 ⤖ Towards Unitary Thinking

I

Shen Hui tells us: "The void no longer exists for those who
have seen their self-nature." (Jacques Gernet, p. 43.) Let us
adjust this translation, which is hardly acceptable literally in
that form: we will say "Void is no longer such for those who
have *recognised themselves* as original mind." No one can "see"

self-nature, which cannot be an object of subject, and, anyhow, it cannot be "his."[1] Obvious as the Master's statement may be to some people, the authority of this awakened sage may be welcome since it is possible to suppose that voidness might be such even to the fully awakened. What is it to these? They do not tell us, for they cannot, since they are it, save—vaguely—that it may be called luminous.[2]

If void has existence only as a concept, equally or, if you care, how much more, must *Nirvana* and *Samsara* be conceptual! They can only exist in dualistic thinking, for in nonduality it goes without saying that they are necessarily one. Therefore, if it is so important for us to see them as one, if we are told in every possible form of words that they are identical and that neither can exist for a moment without the other, it must be in order that we may arrive at that unification of two interdependent concepts. Yet, as concepts, never in all the kalpas that ever were or ever will be could our dualistic machinery see them as one—otherwise than as a third concept—for no two thoughts can occupy consciousness at the same time. So it must be a nondualist seeing that is required of us, and that nondualist resolution of that particular pair of contrasting objects of consciousness can presumably only be effected via a third concept in which they are resolved.

What can that third concept be? No positive concept can be imagined that could combine them. No intermediary

---

[1] Shen Hui himself states: "Si l'espirit (self-nature) pourrait être regardé, il serait alors un *object de la connaissance*." (Jacques Gernet, Chen-Houei, p. 94, n. 15)

[2] "L'activité avec vacuité constante, la vacuité avec activité constante, l'activité avec absence d'être, voilà la vacuité absolue." (ibid., p. 107)

concept—such as "tepid" between "hot" and "cold"—could apply to them, for *Samsara* is necessarily non-*Nirvana*, and *Nirvana* is necessarily non-*Samsara*. The answer, therefore, is evident, logically evident, for being still a matter of dualistic thinking, the laws of logic still apply. The answer is precisely non-*Nirvana* and non-*Samsara*, which is inevitably their identity, for those two negatives of interdependent concepts can only be conceived as one and the same negation, called void.

As I have explained elsewhere, Nirvana is the negative of the supposed duality, and Samsara is the positive, and whenever a negative and a positive are combined, as in the superimposition of two films, they mutually complete and annul one another, leaving a featureless blank, or a void. Analytically regarded, the negative loses its negativity, which is cancelled by the positive, and the positive loses its positivity, which is cancelled by the negative. In fact they become non-negative and non-positive.

Then we are left with a single concept, that of voidness, still a concept, but one which is rather special, for its contrasting element, or "opposite" in duality is non-void—and in apprehending the somewhat evident identity of void and non-void, which is the *negation of both void and non-void*—we reach the unitary vision which is whole-mind and that pure subjectivity which is the awakened state.

II

These so-called dualities are rather counterparts that complete one another and, by completing one another, at the same time cancel one another out as separate entities, and, annihilating one another, leave a mutual negative.

That mutual negative is their resolution, and since conceptually we cannot know it, we have to leave it at that and indicate it by a term such as voidness.

Neither *Nirvana* nor *Samsara* is as an object (a thing): each is a mode of seeing: both are subjective, aspects of subjectivity confronting one another, and their resolution, voidness, is an attempted description from dualism of pure consciousness, in itself known to be resplendent, whose subjective aspect produces dualistic manifestation.

Therein they are one; therefrom, reflected by *skandhas*, they are seen conceptually as dual.

That is why, as objects (thoughts), they could never be united, and why, as subjectivity, they could never be divided.

III

What has been said regarding *Nirvana* and *Samsara* applies equally to non-manifestation and manifestation. They also are subjective, contrasting modes of seeing, inseparable as subjectivity, but forever apart though interdependent when regarded dualistically as two objects of consciousness.

The same applies to non-being and being, and to any two concepts that imply not-seeing and seeing. It applies also, of course, to not-seeing and seeing themselves, which are apart as two thoughts which require a see-er and something not-seen or seen, but they are united as pure see-ing.

To us the most important of these pairs of contrasting interdependent counterparts may seem to be subject and object, for they include everything, and we know from the Masters that their unification in mind is awakening. In what way can they be different?

Absolute Absence

Regarded as subject and object, two thoughts, two concepts, each in turn is an object of consciousness, both are objects, even that one called subject and apparently acting as such. As long as they are so regarded they must necessarily remain apart. But when that object called subject becomes (since it can never be seen as) subjectivity its fellow object, whether a jug or an abstract idea, is thereby also a see-ing—for there is no such thing as an object anywhere in the cosmos: that is just the subjectivity of mind that has been dualistically interpreted as a jug or as an abstract idea. But no interpretation is anything but dualistic imagination: the interpretation is phantasy and in itself the apparent *perception* is just *perceiving*—that is the subjective aspect of pure consciousness which we can only describe as void, just as we seek to indicate the objective notion of things by the word suchness.

There can be little doubt that when a sage such as Huang Po tells us that the sudden perceiving of subject-and object-as-one reveals the truth, he means just what he says, i.e. a pure instantaneous subjective intuition in which unity is revealed. But there is also the methodical approach—if I may be allowed to call it so—of which I have spoken in seeking to clarify the vital message of the Diamond Sutra.

This can be perceived via the Buddha's formula, and most clearly via Shen Hui's laconic—he was generally laconic—version of it. It is the *absence of* the absence of subject and object as phenomena that is the ultimate truth that awakens.

In detail: subject is negative, object is positive. As interdependent counterparts the negative is necessarily non-positive (non-object) and the positive necessarily non-negative (non-subject). Their reunion is perceived when we know that the truth lies in the absence (*wu*), the negation of this dual absence, for then they are no longer phenomenal: they appear as voidness wherein they are inevitably one and indivisible.

IV

Have we understood this time? Yes? No? Probably both Yes and No, for words can never transfer understanding: they can only open the way for pre-existing knowledge to rise into consciousness in the light of which it is recognised and said to be understood.

Supposing that to be the case, someone may complain that Huang Po, and others, promised that we should be awakened thereby, but are we, and, if not, why not?

Don't you see the answer to that? Your understanding is objective comprehension, just that kind of comprehension which the great Masters sought to avoid by never explaining anything to their disciples and by manoeuvring them rather, at the cost of years, into finally reaching that understanding in themselves, by themselves, but for a sudden stimulus, even a kick in the pants, and once and for all. And that sudden understanding was revelation, for the mind turned over, it was self-generated, and it was pure subjective understanding whereby they instantaneously recognised themselves as impersonal consciousness and nothing else whatsoever. I speak of *sambhodi*, of full awakening, of complete *insight,* and not of that opening of the mind, a purely phenomenal manifestation, in time, which can be attained by the manipulation of the psyche of people who have understood little and in whom identification is still intact. This latter is not an end, but a beginning.

If the Masters eschewed objective understanding, why seek it? If it is a hindrance, why urge it? The answer is that we must, that we have no alternative, for we have no fully awakened Masters to shepherd us to the fold. If we do not seek that which we can find—objective understanding—we have nothing, and we do not know what to look for. Our way must be to gain that comprehension, and then to transform it into subjective understanding whereby we recognise ourselves in a flash as subjectivity itself, and the apparent universe as the phantasy or dreamed object of that via our apparent selves.

And the way? That is known as the *Prajnaparamita,* and the Buddha taught it, all the great Dhyana Masters taught it, and, obscure as indeed it is, as liable to misinterpretation and inadequate interpretations as, alas, it is, it is the eternal signpost pointing to the ever-open Gateway of that which is NOT.

Tsung-Mi characterises Shen Hui's teaching as: "The one character *chih* is the gateway to all secrets." Dr. Suzuki translates *chih* as "*prajna*-intuition," and Han Shan tells us categorically that by the word *prajna* the Buddha wished us to understand "subject," so we arrive at subject-intuition or *intuition of subjectivity.* That then is the key of the open Gate. And how wide it stands open when the key is placed in the lock!

Note: The non-existence of particularities—*wu wu* in Chinese, *neti neti* is Sanskrit, meaning Not this, Not that, Not any thing whatsoever (as an object) is the last signpost on the Way.

67 ·– *Syllogistically*

You cannot reach non-duality by means of a logical syllogism: you can bring the interdependent counterparts into correlation, but there will always remain a gap that cannot logically be bridged, for logic is based on dualistic thinking. Duality and non-duality belong to different modes. The jump is from this to the other shore: it is the *paramita*, the going beyond.

Logical thinking can only lead to the brink, and that surely is its most precious function.

Form is the seeing of form: it has no independent existence.
Form as the object of seeing is inexistent.
The thought itself of form is the seeing of form.

Form is the seeing of form,
Void is the non-seeing of form, or the seeing of void.
The seeing of form and the non-seeing of form are subjective seeing or subjectivity.

Therefore the seeing of form is the seeing of void, and the seeing of void is the seeing of form. For both are nothing but pure see-ing, form and void being objective interpretations.
There are no objects.

The dreamed object cannot establish by logic that he is the dreamer, but if he could realize it he would be awake:

For the dreamer is the dreaming, and the dreaming is the dream, the dream is the dreaming, and the dreaming is the dreamer.

68 ·- Form and Void

The longer *Prajnaparamita* Sutra states that "Apart from form there is no void; apart from void there is no form." This appears to mean that form is necessary in order that there may be void, and that void is necessary in order that there may be form.

As concepts this is evident, for void is the absence of form, and form is the absence of void, and neither part of an interdependent pair of concepts can exist, or appear to exist, without the other.

In fact, however, we may understand that neither exists—for both are objects, and the absence of one interdependent object requires the absence of the other. As subjectivity—the void of *Prajna*—they are one, or potential as a pair, and subjectivity objectivises both together or neither, since all objectivisation is via the *skandhas* and dualist.

Where Is Reality?

As the Hindu philosophers found long ago, at the end of human vision there lie three things, which are three aspects of one thing, one thing which can be experienced in three modes—Being, Consciousness and Bliss, known in their Sanskrit form as *Sat-Chit-Ananda*. We can see no further and no path leads beyond.

The Upanishadic method, according to the remarkably qualified Swami Tapasyananda, is that *Sat-Chit-Ananda* are just the negation of their opposites or the affirmation of the absence of their opposites. That implies that they are a manifestation of Non-being, of Unconsciousness and of Non-bliss (or suffering).

This, indeed, we have already understood—that positive manifestation is only the reverse aspect of the negative, which as such always has precedence. It shows also that even *Sat-Chit-Ananda* are phenomenal (in case we doubted it), the noumenal state—if state it can be called—being the negation, or absence, of both, which is the void of subjectivity or what we seek to indicate by the term Pure Consciousness.

Of that, nothing whatsoever can ever be *known*.

There is no place for "Reality" in this picture.

69 ⟿ *"No-Mind Speaking"*

Few of the awakened sages tell us anything of the nature of whole-mind, beyond describing it as void—which is the objective aspect of it as seen by self-identified humanity. But there is one remarkable Master of Ch'an, outstanding in the clarity and vigour of his speech, who gives us some precious information, vague as that inevitably must be.

He is Tsung Kao, 1089-1163, and we owe his words to Mr. Chang Chen Chi in his excellent book called *The Practice of Zen*—somewhat unhappily named since the book is refreshingly concerned exclusively with the original Ch'an doctrine in China. I say this without intended reflection on Japanese Zen, but because it seems to me essential, in our Western interests, to preserve the distinction. If commerce and propaganda find it necessary to force the term Zen on all forms of *Dhyana* where the buying public is concerned, that must not be allowed to influence serious students of the teaching of the Buddha.

But in quoting Tsung Kao I am going to take liberties with the surely excellent translation so kindly offered us, and that because it is given, as usual, as an objective description. An objective description of pure Mind or our "original nature," sometimes called "self-mind," and here "no-mind" (*wu hsin*), makes nonsense, for mind cannot see itself or be seen, but only experienced, and I know of no reason to suppose that Chinese pictograms could make the distinction, since they are innocent of grammar.

"If we want to grasp it," he says, "it runs away from us, but if we cast it away it continues to be there all the time."

In itself that clearly means that we cannot make an object of it, since it is ourself, and we cannot make an object of this which we are.

"We, the originally vast, serene, and marvellous mind are all pure and illuminatingly all-inclusive. Nothing can hinder us: we are as free as the firmament.

"We are like the sun shining in the blue sky—clear and bright, unmovable and immutable, neither increasing nor decreasing. In all daily activities we illumine all places and shine out from all things.

"This mind that we are is vast and expansive like space itself . . . The wonder of the effortless mind naturally and spontaneously reacts to all conditions without any obstacle.

"We do not adhere to anything, but are natural and spontaneous at all times and in all circumstances . . . We who observe our body and mind see them as magic shadows or as a dream. Nor do we abide in this magic or dreamlike state . . . When we reach this point then we can be considered as having arrived at the true state of No-mind."

If indeed Tsung Kao meant to offer this as an objective description, for some good purpose of his own, I apologize to him, but I cannot feel that he would scold me very hard today (though as late as the twelfth century he might have given me thirty blows or a kick in the pants), for in this form his wise words are truly enlightening, much more so than as scholastic dogmatising of which we have so much and which in general means so little to us.

I offer no other comment. Commentary would spoil it. It is to be read as if spoken by ourself. It is to be respoken by ourself. It is to be realized that it is in very truth ourself speaking.

Note: This vacuous old void we hear so much about as *an object* does not sound so gloomy inside?

70 ~ The Mechanism of Duality

I. The Subjective Solution

Subjectivity manifests (objectivises), and we, identified subjects (subjects identified with objects; see II), see, hear, feel, taste, smell, know.

We see lightness and darkness,
We hear sound and silence,
We feel pleasure and pain,
We taste sweetness and sourness,
We smell odour and freshness,
We know good and bad (discrimination applied to each category).

All are subjectivity manifesting, all are we, identified subjects, interpreting the experience of subjectivity in ourselves-as-subjectivity (which is all we *are*).

There *is* no experiencer, there *is* nothing experienced, there *is* only an experiencing—and that is subjectivity manifesting.

Absolute Absence

There *is* no subject, there *is* no object. There is only subjectivity.

II. *Analytic*

(a) Subjectivity manifests, and we, unidentified subjects, experience *Nirvana* (negative), perceived via *skandhas*.
(b) Subjectivity manifests, and we, identified subjects, experience *Samsara* (positive), perceived via senses.

(b) is a sensorial interpretation of (a).
Both are subjectivity manifesting via a sentient object of subjectivity, whose sentiency is subjectivity itself.

Subjectivity manifests, and we, unidentified subjects, experience non-dually (negatively) via *skandhas*.
Subjectivity manifests, and we, identified subjects, experience dually (positively) via senses.

Both are subjectivity manifesting via a sentient object of subjectivity.

Subjectivity manifests, and we, unidentified subjects, experience non-manifestation (negative) via *skandhas*.
Subjectivity manifests, and we, identified subjects, experience manifestation (positive) via senses.
Subjectivity manifests, and we, unidentified subjects, experience as subject (negative) via *skandhas*.
Subjectivity manifests, and we, identified subjects, experience as objects (positive) via senses.

All are subjectivity manifesting via its sentient objects.

All are interpretations, via its sentient objects, of subjectivity manifesting.

Each pair of interdependent counterparts is one in pure subjectivity.

All duality is *interpretation of unity* or non-duality.

This is subjective understanding—understanding via subject.

Objective understanding—understanding via objects, methodical and by logical syllogism, cannot reach the truth, it can only lead to the brink of the void that separates duality from non-duality. It requires a leap to the other shore, a leap which will still be from objectivity to subjectivity.

71 ·~ The Transmission of Truth

It is a sad and extraordinary fact that people of the present day seem psychologically unable to comprehend any thesis that is not expounded in an elaborate architectural construction of verbiage.

A concentrated expression of any thesis is regarded as an "aphorism" which is put aside as inadequate exposition and best ignored.

Yet, as every sage has known, such discursive expositions kill the truth they are intended to convey. Truth is suffocated in a haystack of verbal disquisition, and is born dead.

Living truth cannot be transmitted wrapped up in verbiage, for it cannot be *transmitted* factually at all. It can only be called up by appropriate indication in the mental apparatus of another, and, for that, suggestion, brief, stimulating, and spontaneous, alone can succeed.

The Expression of Truth

The reason why we, or even Sages, cannot—must not or cannot—express what we, they, have understood by intuition, is that by doing so, or even by trying to do so, we, they, would thereby turn it into an object—which *could not* be it. For the ultimate truth is necessarily purely subjective—that is pure subjectivity.

An eye cannot see itself, and
Truth cannot express itself,
Because, being non-duality,
It cannot be conveyed dualistically
As the object of a subject.

We try to convey it, directly; the Sages occasionally did so, but by symbol and implication. But all that can ever be done is to open a way whereby, summoned, it may rise into the consciousness in which already it lies sleeping.

72 ⸱⁓ Looking in the Right Direction

Seeing everything as "Mind itself" does not mean seeing objects as Mind. That is still looking in the wrong direction, mistaking East for West.

"Seeing everything as Mind itself" means rather "As Mind itself, seeing everything": it is a displacement of the see-er from being a see-er of pseudo-objects to being "Mind itself." The see-er was an object himself, and so a pseudo-see-er.

Let me put it another way: seeing everything as "Mind itself" does not mean seeing everything, that is objects, in a different manner. It means ceasing to see objects (everything) at all, by ceasing to look, to be at all, and re-becoming "the Mind itself" which is what, and all one really is, ever was, or ever could be.

Seeing objects as Mind, or Mind as objects, is still the dualistic performance of subject looking at object, and it matters not which way round it may be done. What is being required of us is the non-dual vision implicit in self-recognition as "Mind itself," which is just pure consciousness. Therein see-er and seen are one and there is only a see-ing.

Judgements

All comparison is based on memory, and memory is an image based on engrams. It follows that all judgement, evaluation, is an interpretation of images, for even the present is already a memory by the time we have seized it.

Therefore the unending process of finding things "good" or "not so good" is a work of imagination. Would it not be futile indeed to suppose that such judgements, that is any and all judgements, could have any absolute existence or value?

73 · Restatement

The aim of all religions, explicit in Buddhism, Vedanta, implicit in some others, is recovery of our real nature by awakening from the living-dream, called *wu* or *satori* in China and Japan.

The method is recognising that which we really are by understanding that which we are not, or that we are not what we think that we are.

The dissolution of the erroneous identification automatically leaves us as in fact we have been from before the moment at which we fell victims to the dualistic interpretation.

This very simple situation having been grasped, all we have to do is sufficiently thoroughly to apprehend that we are NOT ("not" implying *everything* our intellect has been conditioned to assume that we are in its interpretation of sensorial perceptions). By knowing what we are not, we are left with the understanding of what we are.

The Marx Bros.

Movement creates Space in which it may occur, and Time by which it may be recognised.

Time cannot exist without Movement to measure, and Space in which Movement may take place.

Space cannot exist without Movement to render it perceptible, and Time by which its duration, which is its existence, may be observed.

74 ·- The True Sense of "Intuition"

Thoughts "arise" in the conditioned aspect of consciousness. In the interval between thoughts consciousness shines clear. To the time-sense this interval is imperceptible, and only intuition has the requisite rapidity to utilise these intervals.

But we should understand this correctly. The intervals between thoughts are not brief glimpses of a world surrounding us, or messages from such a world.

Consciousness itself is that world, and we are consciousness. Thoughts arising in consciousness arise in us. The intervals in that process reveal us as we are: we can know ourselves then as pure consciousness, i.e. as all that we really are. It is precisely to this realization that we have to awaken from our living-dream. "In-tuition" (looking within) is really looking from within.

Imagining ourselves as what our senses lead us to suppose, we tend to think that intuitions squeeze through the thought-intervals from somewhere or other and reach our brain or our mind or whatever name we give our cognitive faculties. That is identification, and it is the nonsense of identification.

These flashes are moments of being ourselves—for thoughts conceal us from ourselves, and we cannot be ourselves when thoughts intervene. For thoughts are manifestation, phenomenal, part of the dream, and are in relation with the psycho-somatic apparatus that we regard as ours, if not as us. Thoughts arising in the conditioned aspect of consciousness are related to the dream-figure with which we are erroneously identified in the dream of living.

Intuition, on the other hand, is our impersonal "self" (using the term as Vedantists do), and when we recognise this we become it for the duration of the apprehension. We are just being ourselves, what we are when we are no longer "we." The *awareness* of all thoughts is we as consciousness, but they are then our objects, whereas intuitions are subjective and consciousness itself.

The "interval between" is pure impersonal I.

75 ·~ The Buddha's Formula in Brief

An object appears to exist;
But it is not (because it is an object);
Nevertheless it is (as an objectivisation of subjectivity).

Note: An objectivisation of subjectivity is subjectivity.

The Buddha's Formula in Full

"X" is a phenomenon;

Phenomena are objects, and objects do not exist as such; but they are not "the void of annihilation";

For phenomena *are* as the expression of noumenon, objects *are* as the manifestation of the subjective aspect of pure consciousness via *skandhas*, so that their suchness is subjectivity which is our experience of pure consciousness.

Note: The subject that perceives objects and the objects perceived are both phenomenal. Neither exists; but the negation of both, of non-object and of non-subject (the absence of dual absences) is the "Void of Prajna" or subjectivity, so that the perceiving alone IS, and that is their suchness.

They ARE only, even as suchness, when WE perceive.

"WE" are all sentient beings.

76 — Another Way of Saying It

Things have no self-nature: their self-nature is void.

Void is the self-nature of things, that which they are when "they" are not.

That is why form (things) is void and void is form, and why there is no form without void, and no void without form.

Another Way of Doing It

Unreality is the seriality created by the time-concept, and which I have called "horizontal" seeing, i.e. one-damn-thing-after-another.

Freed from the time-concept—seriality reintegrated, the succession of objects (objects apparently developing, cause and effect) reunified, and...

Freed also from the space-concept—for Time and Space are inseparable—the seen object becomes "real"—for it is seen in the manner I have called "vertical."

Intemporal and in-formal, the supposed object has re-become subjectivity and re-found its only reality as pure see-ing.

Note: Liberation from the Space-time concepts is transference from objectivising into "subjectivising"—or the famous "leap."

Here "objectivising" means seeing everything as an object, or objectively, and "subjectivising" means seeing everything as from subject or subjectively.

It can also be called seeing noumenally.

The former was called the "Guest" position in China, as opposed to the "Host" position, or that of the "Minister" as opposed to that of the "Prince," or, by other Masters, the "functional" position in contrast to that of "Principal" or "Potentiality."

77 ᐟ *Bodhi, Svaha!*

I

The Ch'an Master Chin awakened Wu Wen (Mumon) by telling him: "To understand this, face South to see the Great Bear." This means, "Turn your back on the object" (on objectivity).

But if we look in the opposite direction—that is subjectivity looking at itself—all that we shall behold is voidness. That is what Han Shan calls the Void of *Prajna,* absolute void, which, he also tells us, the Buddha wished us to understand as subject. It has also been well-termed Absolute Absence, by Tetsugen.

Absolute Absence

Meng Shan expressed it like this: "Suddenly and a
I recognised myself." Clearly it is not a case of lookin
object, but of self-recognition.

How does this process work? In the first place the metaphysical aspect of mind has to be sufficiently developed to
take over the control of the psycho-somatic apparatus. In all
ordinary cases this is a matter of many years, not of learning
but of experience, for our system of "education" is exclusively
devoted to developing the samsaric ego-ridden mentality.
Consequently it requires a *metanoesis* or *paravritti* (turning
over) to awaken the nirvanic aspect of mind, which can occur
without its being recognised as such; but, recognised or not,
the process of bringing it to maturity is long and only
depends indirectly on thought. This gradual development is
phenomenal and subject to time.

The intemporal awakening, *Bodhi*, or *Sambodhi*, of
which *Anuttara-samyak-sambodhi*, the complete, unexcelled
Enlightenment of the Buddha is a further development,
may be regarded as a final transfer of control of the psycho-
somatic apparatus from the samsaric to the nirvanic aspect of
mind. The Chinese termed the latter the original or self-
mind, the "self"-mind meaning not personal but subjective.
The phenomenon is then said to be "liberated," which does
not mean that the apparent individual can do whatever he
likes for the rest of his life, for his phenomenal aspect remains
subject to the pattern according to which he is being "lived,"
but that he has recognised himself as subjectivity and, as
such, is perfectly free from the illusions of the living dream.
It could also be made to mean that subjectivity is liberated
from its identification and apparent limitation, which would
involve the absurdity of objectivising subject.

This process of transference of control, from apparent
objectivity to permanent subjectivity, is the famous leap or

jump, sometimes called "into the void," which it evidently is, since the "Void of Prajna" is just subjectivity. It is also referred to as the step off the top of the "hundred-foot pole," the latter being objective understanding which has to be abandoned before subjective understanding can be reached.

But the best-known description of this essential turning-over of the mind, transfer of control, or leap over an abyss, is the famous paramita, or so-called going to the "other shore," epitomised in the highly-lauded mantram—*Gate, gate, paragate, parasamgate, Bodhi, Svaha!*, which is usually translated for us, "Gone, gone, gone over, gone right over, Awakening, Svaha!" ("Svaha" being untranslatable, since there is no word for a blessing in English or French, and our greetings are all either vulgar or comic). This mantram has been discussed elsewhere, and it was pointed out that there is nothing to have gone over anything, but merely a go*ing*. In fact, however, it should surely be a com*ing*, for the mind is turning, or leaping, not away from but back towards itself. It is a leap inwards not outwards. Without doubting the technical accuracy of the current translations one may point out that *gate* can mean "come" as well as "gone," so that the sense of the mantram could be, and surely should be, "Coming, coming, coming over, coming right over, Awakening, Well-come!" Used as a mantram, it is better left in the original, though it is necessary to know the sense before using it.

The essential point here is that it is not on the other shore that there has to be a landing, but on the hither shore, for the shore opposite to objectivity is the shore in question, and that shore is "within" rather than "without." We must leap through ourselves, not away from ourselves. As a Chinese Master (Tsung Kao) put it, "you feel as if you had stumbled over a stone and *stepped upon your own nose*." When Wu Wen realized that, Ursa Major being in the Northern hemisphere, he was required to turn around in the direction opposite to objectivity, i.e. towards subjectivity which, when looking at itself, can only see voidness, he found that he was awake. Han Shan, a relatively modern but authentically awakened Ch'an Master (1546-1623) explains this leap inwards, rather than outwards, from another angle. He says: "If one breaks through the nest of the Eight Consciousnesses, and with one great leap passes right through, then there is nothing more for him to attain....Why? Because if the Eight Consciousnesses are not broken through, whatever one sees and does are merely works of the samsaric consciousness and senses." The eight consciousnesses, corresponding to each of the senses, cognition, egoity, and what is called the Witness in Vedanta, cover all that we have been conditioned to regard as the psychic aspect of ourselves. So, if we leap through that we must leap through ourselves, not away from ourselves.

From looking outwards we turn our gaze inwards, but this does not mean perceiving objects mentally instead of via our senses: it means that we as subjectivity suddenly turn from objectivising (in any direction) to subjectivising, which is turning the objectivising process and energy in upon ourselves. What we then behold is no longer the objective world, *samsara*, but the subjective world, *nirvana*, but we see nothing—precisely because we are subjectivity looking at itself and only seeing what we have to call voidness or absence. Remember, *we are still looking*, but in the right direction at last, and we see that we, as subjectivity, are what we are looking at—and that is no thing. *Then we know that we are not.*

It is this act of "looking" that is the "jumping," and it is still phenomenal. At that moment we realize that we are void, that void is subjectivity, and that subjectivity is us—not us as individual selves but as all sentient beings, not as any sort of sentient being but as sentient *being* as such.

That is the negative way, that of the *Prajnaparamita*, that is why we must know that we are not in order that we may understand in what manner we can be, that is the Buddha's formula in the Diamond Sutra, that is the explanation of the doctrine enshrined in the Heart Sutra, that is landing on the hither shore to which we return from objectivising in the wilderness of the dream-world of *samsara*. And that is why no objects *are* otherwise than as imagined by our phenomenal faculties which themselves are mind-only.

What is the result of that leap from objectivity to subjectivity, that turning-over of the mind? Master Kao Feng tells us: "At that moment my doubts were suddenly broken up, I felt as if I had jumped out of a trap. All the puzzling koans of the Masters and the Buddhas and all the different issues and events of both present and ancient times became transparently clear to me. Henceforth *all things were settled; nothing under the sun remained but peace.*"

II

To the foregoing descriptive account, designed to promote objective understanding, let us add a more analytical treatment of the actual process, which may help towards its transformation into subjective understanding.

Phenomenal mind functions within dimensional limitations, and its movement can be said to occur on a horizontal plane. It can "look" inwards or outwards, forwards or backwards, but "horizontally" only. Consequently its looking inwards, in opposition to outwards via the senses, is inevitably imaginative and conceptual. This, as has been said, does not lead to the jump from objectivity to subjectivity. Subject and object are on the same "horizontal" plane, whereas subjectivity is to be regarded as also perpendicular or

Absolute Absence

"vertical." That looking in an unfamiliar direction is the actual "jump." That, also, is the difficulty, for the phenomenal aspect of mind does not know how to "look" in a new direction and indeed cannot, for in so-doing it ceases to function.[1] It is necessary, however, to "look" in order to leap; otherwise the mind will continue its "horizontal" functioning, but the "looking" ceases the moment the leap is taken into what appears as a void. In that instant see-er and seen disappear as apparently such, and there is only a see-ing. That see-ing is vertical, nirvanic, subjective, and in whole-mind. And then we perceive mountains and rivers once more, but differently, for now and henceforward seeing has a further dimension and phenomena are recognised as subjectivity.

This is why there is a *solution de continuité* between *samsara* and *nirvana*, why a "leap" over an "abyss" is inevitable. One Ch'an Master—probably Shen Hui—went so far (for a Chinese sage) as to *explain* that the reason why a gradual attainment of *nirvana* is impossible is that *samsara* and *nirvana* are of different orders of being and that consequently no bridge can lead from the one to the other. What has been said here merely expresses this in our Western idiom. It is also, perhaps, the perfect justification of *Tsung*, literally the Principle, as opposed to *Chiao*, the Doctrine, the former exclusively applied to Ch'an, the latter to all other forms of Hinayana and Mahayana Buddhism, and encourages one to believe that the realization, i.e. the

[1] According to Hsu Yun, the Bodhisattva Avalokiteshvara, advised by Mansjuri, developed the bodhi-mind not by "looking" but by "hearing," which he regarded as the most suitable for mankind. This confirms that the "leap" is phenomenal and that it takes place as a result of a sensual activity. (See Charles Luk's *Chan and Zen Teaching*, pp 89-92.)

experiencing, of this was indeed the Buddha's ultimate message for those who were able to understand.

78 ·- Débris: Space and Time

No thing in Space-time exists as such. Space-time is "horizontal" (the *serial time-dimension*).
All objectivisation is in space-time.

❦

All the "impermanency" talk, birth, decay, death, etc. is what we should simply understand as the *seriality of time*, which is illusory. *Its unreality is just its seriality.*

❦

Subjectivity seems to be pure consciousness *subject to time*.

❦

Suchness is just the time-less (vertical, subjective) aspect of anything so called.

❦

"Opposites" are very exactly warp and woof—running in contrary directions on one plane surface. Seen from above (a further dimension) you see the piece of stuff they comprise.

❦

Whole-Mind

All desires represent a craving for *the essential deprivation,* which we seek to gratify vicariously.

79 ·– Vertical "Vision," 2

Objects can be said to be perceived in a horizontal space-time dimension.

Subjectivity can be said to be vertical seeing.

In the vertical (noumenal) dimension phenomena (objects) are projected, and are seen on the duodimensional horizontal plane-surface.

Objects are perceived serially (in space and in time) as interpretation by conditioned mind of sensorial impressions of a perception presented by the *skandha* mechanism, this perception before interpretation having merely the characteristics of essential contrast, i.e. light and shade (visual), sharp and flat (audition), light and heavy (tactile), delicate and pungent (odorific), sweet and sour (gustatory). From this contrasting appearance, called dualism, the senses provide conditioned mind with the means of creating objects.

Subjectivity is a name chosen to indicate pure consciousness as it *appears* when subject to space and time. It is also an objectivisation as such.

Subjectivity is vertical "vision," pure consciousness before suffering transformation by the *skandha* mechanism, but subject to space and time when objectivised via the senses. Then of course, it is illusory: in itself it remains transcendent to space and time.

Sentient beings, which are objects (phenomena) as such, ARE pure subjectivity and nothing else. Regarded horizontally, in space-time, they are phenomena (interpretations) only, because then they are *being regarded*—subjectively, of course, but via objects, which condition is known as "identification." Vertically they cannot be so regarded, which would automatically make them objects, but they can be experienced subjectively as We.

It could never be possible to state this in a completely logical manner, because thought itself is the process of objectivisation. Therefore any attempt at explanation immediately transforms subjectivity into an object. Only the first person singular or plural, "I" or "we," alone or followed by "am" or "are," can ever express subjectivity as such. Even then it can only be *spoken:* it cannot be *heard* subjectively.

80 — Absolute Absence

I

Wu, No-thingness, Void is just no *thing—non-objectivity.* It is therefore subjectivity. It is void simply because all "things" whatsoever are objective, and it is that which is not objective. Being subjectivity, in so far as it "is" at all, it can only "be" the "act" of subjectivity looking at itself via us, such "act" being purely theoretical, since there could not be anything seen. The term "void" and its synonyms alone can give an indication of this process of an eye looking at itself, and consequently seeing nothing.

II

When one says "I am not," that means "I am void," for I am subjectivity and nothing else—and that is nothingness *when "looked at" by itself.* The same words can mean that I am not as a phenomenal individual, so that either in *samsara* or in *nirvana* I am not and nothing is, and I am absolute absence. Since "things" depend upon me, they are absence also. The only sense in which anything can "be" is as perceived by us who are only pure subjectivity which itself is no-mind.

III

One should clearly understand that subjectivity "is" not either, but is only a method of indicating no-mind as it can be apprehended by us who perceive manifestation subject to the notions of space and time. This cannot be stated syllogistically, for "we" are only the apperceiving in question ourselves.

All this that I have said, meaningless to many, can only serve as a clue or an indication to those who may be ready to use it as such.

81 ⁓ *Absolute Presence*

"The void is fundamentally without spatial dimensions." (Huang Po, Wan Ling Records, p. 93.)[1]

[1] *Ed. note:* From *The Zen Teaching of Huang Po* by John Blofeld.

An object is spatial. But no thing really exists spatially, therefore no object really exists.

Why? Because No-Mind cannot be subjected to limitation, either spatial or temporal, and so can have no objective existence, which is why nothing whatsoever, not even No-Mind, can be—otherwise than as pure subjectivity.

Note: No-Mind = One Mind = Whole-Mind.

82 ᐟ Chih

"Why this talk of *seeing* into your own nature?" (Huang Po)

"Subjectivity," as a word, or a thought, is an object. Using it is creating an object in order to describe that which is not an object. No doubt that is why the Masters did not use it—if its counterpart existed in Chinese.[1]

But, without Masters, *we need it.* It alone can turn our minds in the right direction. Like Shen Hui's *Chih*, it is the Gateway to all secrets.

"Subjectivity" should never be thought of as any thing. If it is thought of it should be regarded simply as the resolution of the duality subject-object, and be left nameless.

[1] The term "Mind" often means subjectivity, and nothing else, in the texts, but being an almost colloquial expression it carries a purely objective sense to a reader who has not already understood. "No-Mind," its counterpart, even if it tends to take the reader out of objectivity, does not point directly in the right direction either—at any rate to us. The Chinese words *hsin* and *wu-hsin* are even more general and ambiguous, as technical terms, than their equivalents in our language. The term "One-Mind" comes nearer to direct suggestion.

The resolution of *every duality is nameless,* and is that. For no non-duality can be a thing or an object.

Once understood, it should not be thought of at all, nor sought, nor "looked" at, for it is that We which we, as we, can never see.

As a word it is only a pointing finger, rather the *pointing* of a finger, not a finger pointing at anything or at nothing—unless at itself as us—a pure pointing in an invisible dimension.

Perhaps as a word it means too much. If so it hides its own light, blocks its own path, nullifies its own existence.

We must not let it mean anything whatever, but just produce a stimulus, an impulse, pull a trigger, touch off a charge, release an energy *in the essential direction.*

Let us rather call it *Chih,* for the literal meaning of that we may not know.

83 ·— *The Wave-Mechanism Symbol of Transmigration*

The late Nyanatiloka Thera explains transmigration by the analogy of the undulatory motion of a wave. In view of the Buddhist denial of any species of entity this analogy is of particular interest.

The wind of desire instigates a vertical movement *in situ,* limited by the force of inertia. This vertical movement is transmitted—by some such process as displacement—to the adjoining body of water, and from that to the next, and so on until the initial impulse (karmic) is exhausted or until the succession of bodies reaches a rising shore on which the vertical mass breaks down for lack of the resistance of further bodies of water. Superficial observers of this process mistake the vertical motion *sur place* for a horizontal motion, and think that a body of water, called a wave, is actually moving, swept on by the wind, towards the shore until it disintegrates thereon.

Is this a generally accurate image of the process of trans-migration? Each "body of water," or so-called wave, here symbolises a birth-and-death or "incarnation," in its vertical rise and fall, and its fall transmits the impulse to its successor. But no movement in our time sense—which is "horizon-tal"—actually takes place: there is merely a vertical rising and falling. The only transmission is of an impulse by pressure; no entity exists or passes, no quality, no quantity, nothing specif-ic, just an energy—of increasing or decreasing velocity. The wind of craving maintains or increases this pressure, and when its own force fails the whole process lapses and relative immobility returns, the multitudinous "wave-bodies" re-becoming just water.

Superficial observers think that the transmigration of an entity takes place in a space-time dimension, but in this image only an impulse is transmitted from wave-body to wave-body, producing what is from a horizontal view-point a static effect. And the wind of desire alone brings about such transmission, and such "static" effect, which is "life" between "birth" and "death."

Is this illustration adequate? Any kind of transmigration must necessarily be *samsaric,* that is phenomenal, for noumenon could not be involved, but it would have to be admitted that selected wave-bodies could by reintegration with still water (awakening or enlightenment) be freed from the wind of desire, and so be eliminated from the process, which is an occurrence for which the illustration does not allow.

Absolute Absence

That, however, may not invalidate the analogy, for transmigration (or reincarnation) cannot really exist (as indeed the
Maharshi formally stated), that is to say it can only appear to
exist phenomenally (in *samsara*). But Awakening, which is
said to end transmigration, is not phenomenal and should not
be phenomenally perceptible, since the awakened state is not
as such in the "horizontal" direction of measurement and
should not directly effect any *samsaric* process. If it is necessary to arrive at a satisfactory understanding of the transmigration phenomena so universally accepted, as such, by the
Masters, this seems to be a valuable suggestion and is stated
by Nyanatiloka, a Theravadin, as "factual."

84 ⹊ Science and Soda

Some people see a profound significance in the fact that
modern science is busy establishing, in its dualistic analysis of
the universe of our living dream, a resemblance to the non-
dual universe known to the totally awakened, and vaguely
described by them.

Since these descriptions of the awakened, in so far as they
are descriptions, must necessarily be dualistic also, it is hardly surprising that the two should resemble one another—for
what the awakened see, when they look objectively, are
"mountains and rivers" as before—though no doubt with a
difference, which is what they seek to describe.

But the truth, which they cannot describe—since description, even thought itself, are necessarily objective—being
pure subjectivity is of another order or dimension altogether,
so that no sort of comparison could ever be possible (cf. the
Buddha's "comparison" of the virtue ("merits") of *samsaric*

almsgiving and *nirvanic* understanding, in the Diamond Sutra).

That which the awakened see, objectively, are again "mountains and rivers"; that which they see, subjectively, is voidness (an eye looking at itself); and when they desist from "looking"—they ARE, which has been described as *sat-chit-ananda*.

Note: What is the "difference" in what the awakened see after disidentification? "Looking"—subject regarding object—is always the same dualistic process conditioned by space-time limitations. But they *know* that phenomena are unreal, whereas to the rest of us that is at most theoretical only. Moreover they *know* that phenomena are subjectivity, since there is nothing else. To revert to the formula which has always seemed to me the simplest; they know that there is neither see-er nor seen, but only a see-ing. Perhaps that sufficiently suggests the "difference" in their vision of the "mountains and rivers"? Their see-ing, of course, is "pure perception."

85 · Mises au Point

One must know that one is not in order to be able to understand that we are.

As long as one believes that one is, as long as there remains a smouldering ember of this belief, it will be difficult, if not impossible, to apprehend or to experience in what manner we can really be.

⚭

"Every single sight and sound" is an effect of subject-object: no objective effect can appear to exist without a subject-cause (or vice versa).

Therefore "every single sight and sound" is that subject-object integrated in subjectivity.

Subjectivity does not "see" or "hear" any sight or sound: it IS that sight or sound—not as a sight or sound but as a see-*ing* or a hear-*ing*.

❧

"There is absolutely nothing which can be attained." (Huang Po, Wan Ling Record, p. 125.)

"Attainment"—an *object, experienced*, in *time*—represents three modes of unreality, and is therefore a threefold illusion. Three-in-one, for attainment is pure objectivity.

"I assure you that one who comprehends the truth of 'nothing to be attained' is already seated in the sanctuary (*bodhimandala*) where he will gain his Enlightenment." (Huang Po, Wan Ling Record, p. 128.)

There you see: you are sitting pretty! Even though a *bodhimandala* may sound a trifle draughty in these northern climates.

Note: Please don't mistake this comment for sarcasm. Even apart from the authority of Huang Po, who *knew*, is it not evident?

86 ·— Birth-and-Death: The Facts

Karma is an apparent cause that produces an apparent effect in the apparent world of *samsara*.

Rebirth is an apparent occurrence, resulting from the unsatisfied craving of an apparent entity which suffers apparent misery or apparent good-fortune in a time-sequence uninterrupted by intervening apparent deaths—all resulting from the aforesaid apparent actions called *karma*.

All very simple. All rather silly. All utterly unreal. All, at any rate, quite unimportant.

Note: Need anything further be said on this subject? Surely not, but for those who cannot yet see it: "birth-and-death" being unreal, "karma" being unreal, "samsara" itself being unreal, why should the transmigration process require a "real" entity? The argument that there is none, and that therefore transmigration is an inexplicable mystery, since there is nothing to transmigrate, is absurd. It is confusing "reality" and "unreality," *samsara* and *nirvana*.

All things *samsaric* are apparent only, and in *samsara* there are apparent entities, innumerable apparent entities. Trying to make out that they are merely aggregates, bundles of sticks, parts that don't make a whole, is begging the question. It is missing the point, which is that all the factors concerned are equally unreal, so that the unreality of "entities" is not in question at all.

This is treating *samsara* and *nirvana* as though they were one-in-appearance, whereas they are one-in-transcendence: no pair of opposites can ever be one in duality, nor two in non-duality. Nothing transmigrates, for there is nothing to transmigrate, and there is no such reality as transmigration. But in *samsara* any apparent entity might transmigrate—call it consciousness, if you will—but preferably nothing that depends on genetics (heredity). One of these days the psychologists, when they have grown out of their early preconceptions, will tell us exactly what it may be called, and only psychologists are qualified to do so. Meantime let us cease trying to explain something *samsaric* as though it were, or in terms of, something *nirvanic*—which it could not be.

87 ·~ The Fantasy of Enlightenment

"In the true teaching of the Three Vehicles it is clearly explained that the ordinary and Enlightened minds are illusions." (Huang Po, p. 58.)[1]

I fear we talk nonsense about nearly everything, but it seems particularly regrettable that we should do so, so much, and so often, about enlightenment, since that is the aim of all our endeavours, whether we are fully conscious of it or not. Even our best teachers can be heard so modestly to murmur from time to time to the effect that, of course, they themselves are not enlightened.

What absolute rubbish! Of course they are enlightened—if anyone is; and so are you, so am I—if anyone is; every sentient being necessarily is—in so far as the term means anything at all. As an objective state, which is what we are thinking of, nothing of the kind exists or could exist: it is merely that which we are, all that we are. Elsewhere Huang Po tells us: "Our original Buddha-nature is, in highest truth, devoid of any atom of objectivity." And he goes on to say: "It is void, omnipresent, silent, pure: it is glorious and mysterious peaceful joy—and that is all." (Chün Chou Record, p. 35.)[2]

But we don't know it, and knowing it is enlightenment? As phenomena we could never know it. We could only know it by becoming it. And we cannot do that, because we are it. As it, we cannot know it, for knowing is objective understanding—which is phenomenal, and it cannot be understood—for it is just being.

[1] *Ed. Note:* WWW is quoting here from *The Zen Teaching of Huang Po* by John Blofeld.

[2] Ibid.

Regarding it as an object to be attained is insensate. The Buddha himself stated that he had attained nothing whatsoever, and the Masters tell us *ad nauseam* that there is nothing that can be attained. Huang Po says it tirelessly. And with good reason, for it says everything. If we could turn round and face in the right direction, if for only one moment, it should be enough. Attaining, grasping, perceiving (I did not say apperceiving), entering, realizing, conceiving, asking, seeking, finding, reaching, etc., etc. are all possible only when one is turned in the wrong direction. Why? Who is doing any of those things? A pseudo-subject is seeking an object—and neither exists as such.

So how may we speak of enlightenment without talking nonsense? Perhaps we cannot speak at all without talking nonsense, but, if that is so, we may feel that there are nevertheless degrees of nonsense. When we sleep, do we think or talk about being awake in the morning? In the morning we take it for granted that we are awake—for that is our word for the state in which we inevitably are. Yes, we have some recollection of our dreams, and so have the awakened from the living-dream—when they look backwards.

When they look outwards they see what we see (with a difference). When they look inwards they see nothing, for that is the Void (an eye looking at itself). And when they desist from "looking"—they just are. That has been called *sat-chit-ananda*, also universal benediction—for the so-called *bodhi*-mind, enlightenment-mind, inexistent of course, as such, as an object, is pure giving.

The simple word "awakening" suggests all that need be suggested.

88 ⋅~ *That Which Is Not, 2*

When Hui Neng pointed out to the two argumentative monks that the cause of the flapping of the flag was neither the wind nor the flag itself, but the mind that observed them, he left it to them to understand that, though the wind was the *immediate* cause of the flapping, the *ultimate* cause was mind itself.

All phenomena result from an immediate cause, which is the subject of the phenomenal object, and both are phenomenal. Their ultimate cause is always mind—if that is the term chosen to indicate it. But mind is no-mind, for it is not an object: it is pure absence of object. It is absence of both mind and of no-mind.

Things neither exist nor do not exist—for both existence and non-existence are phenomenal. It is this mutual absence of both phenomenal objects—cause-and-effect, subject-and-object—that is their noumenon. To give this a name, thereby making it an object, would be absurd. It is just that which is not.

In order to be understood, the ultimate cause is best thought of as being in another dimension, at right-angles to that of the observed objects. Imagined, phenomena—immediate cause and effect—may be regarded as being "horizontal," and noumenon, ultimate cause, as being "vertical."

89 ⋅~ *Absence, as Defined by Shen Hui*

Wu Nien, Absence-of-thought and its obverse seem to be regarded by Shen Hui as two aspects of one whole, so that in referring to the one he implies the other. It is the "thought in the absence of thought, which is the activity of the Absolute" that he implies. Thought being objectivisation, its obverse and absence must be non-objectivisation.

When he says, "The absence-of-thought is the unique thought of the Absolute" he means that a phenomenal absence, that is an absence of phenomenality, is at the same time the "activity of the Absolute," *is* in fact the "Absolute" which is also the "substance" of the thought. This can only be pure subjective "thought." This gives a definition of absence-of-thought, which is "Thought, which is absence-of-thought, is the activity of the Absolute, and the Absolute is the 'substance' of the thought." This is described as "the foundation of the doctrine."

Wu Nien is also the condition permitting *Y Nien*, which is instantaneous, i.e. intemporal, thought. Again it is made clear that *Wu Nien* is closely associated with *Tsu-jan*, which is translated as "spontaneity" and which is specifically Taoist. It is also the "Buddha-nature," and is equated with *vaçita* in Sanskrit. Since Absence-of-thought is non-objectivity this is evident enough. They are various words for what is ultimately one whole. Absence-of-thought is therefore instantaneous, or spontaneous, thought.

These negative terms are used in a positive sense, in the "vertical" positivity of their negation. *Wu Nien,* and, no doubt, *Wu Hsin,* do not mean just an absence of thought and mind: they are used in the positive sense of the "indeterminate" activity of the Absolute. Absence implies and requires the Presence of that which cannot be named because, named, it would thereby become an object.

All the "Absences" are virtually indications of "Presences," which are their positive counterparts, but these are not the positives of the negative term that is "absent," but of *the absence of that.* They indicate the "vertical" truth which is revealed when the corresponding unreality is negated.

Absolute Absence

Negative terms such as "No-mind" (*Wu-hsin*), "No-thought" (*Wu-nien*) do not just negate their own positives on the same, or "horizontal" plane—"mind" and "thought": it is the mutual negation of these and of their negations that reveals their "vertical" reality which, *not being an object,* cannot be named without thereby becoming that which it is not.

The absence of "mind" and of "thought," and of "no-mind" and "no-thought," on the "horizontal" plane, reveals the void which is non-objective. In describing it also as "the activity of the Absolute, and the Absolute as the "substance of thought" Shen Hui goes further than any other Master in giving us a positive indication of what is meant. It is, of course, once more, the formula of the Tathagata in the Diamond Sutra.

All these "absences" point *directly* at the one vital and ultimate truth (the "foundation of the doctrine") which is the meaning of *prajnaparamita* and the awakening to our "true nature."

Absence of thought is then absolute thought, non-dual and spontaneous.

Shen Hui's formula, "Son absence de prise et de non-prise en est la vraie prise," being virtually untranslatable, can be transposed into another context as "Absence of being and of non-being is true being." Here again the term "absence" carries a "vertical" positive which the form "Neither being nor non-being—that is true being" hardly implies, and for which the form "We neither are nor are not—that is what we truly are" would be better. In short the formula appears to need the implication of the positive of its essential negative, on the "vertical" plane. This, of course, is the Tathagata's formula again.

All this is illustrated by Hui Neng's settlement of the monks' argument over the flag and the wind. Always it is neither the positive nor the negative phenomenal appearance, the immediate cause and its effect, dualistic subject and object, that is the ultimate cause, but mind only, which alone *is* and in which everything appears to occur. Shen Hui's formula is a clarification of the formula of the Diamond Sutra, which, as I have suggested, is probably textually faulty except in one instance.

Shen Hui's formula is in any case just an example of his explanation of the Diamond Sutra formula, when he declares "l'absence même de cette absence des phénomenès d'un moi, de l'autre, des êtres, et de l'age, est le véritable sens de la *gatha* de quatre vers." It is necessarily a double negative (as, indeed, is once given in the text) because a single absence is just the negative aspect of a presence, part of one whole, i.e. "nonbeing" is a form of "being." The truth is clearly the absence of both, i.e. the positive of the mutual negation of what they are and of what they are not. That positive is in the "vertical" dimension, and is the subjective aspect of what is conveniently called One Mind.

This is all very clear once it is "seen," but owing to the manner in which the problem has been presented to us, it has not hitherto been quite evident.

90 — Ex Cathedra

"If people have recourse to a 'method,' that is an error, they cannot obtain deliverance." (Shen Hui, p. 65.)

" '*Prajna*' (Subjectivity) is our true nature." (T'an Ching—the sutra of Hui Neng.)

"*Anuttara-samyak-sambodhi* is called 'The Dharma of Extinction'." (Shen Hui, p. 75.)

"The Buddha-nature is neither being nor non-being."
(Shen Hui, p. 73.)

"*Dhyana* means 'regarding' the basic nature." ("the," not
even "our"—Shen Hui, p. 94.)

"To fix (concentrate) one's mind is an error. Thus the
method of looking at one's mind among the Northern Sect
causes it to defeat its own true ends. If the mind could be
looked-at, it would then be an *object of knowledge*." (Shen
Hui, p. 94, n. 15.)

"Subjectivity is the substance of *samadhi*, and *samadhi* is
the activity of subjectivity." (T'an Ching—the sutra of Hui
Neng.)

"Seeing that one cannot see the absence-of-things (subjectivity) is true seeing, permanent seeing." (Shen Hui, p. 33.)

If *Samsara* is regarded not as a mode of see-ing but as that
which is seen, then *Nirvana is the "vertical" aspect of Samsara.*

91 ·~ Dhyana

I

That which is not objective is not at all.
The only being or existing is being or existing as an object,
For we can know nothing that is not an object.
That is why *anuttara-samyak-sambhodi* is called "The
Dharma of Extinction."
But when all objectivity is totally extinguished,
That which, to us, is not at all, shines like the sun,
For Absolute Absence is pure radiance forever.

II. *Explanatory*

Our whole understanding of being and "isness" is based on objectivity. Nothing that is not an object can appear to have being or to exist for us.

Although that which is not objective has no kind or degree of existence for us, yet this absence must be the source and origin of everything that we know.

As I have explained with regard to "Reality," without objectivity there can be no subject, for there is no object; therefore there cannot be anyone or any thing whatsoever, and so nothing can be or can exist.

92 ⁓ *Adieu*

I

Only objects exist, and nothing can exist that is not an object.

Existence in itself is objective (an objective fact). Both etymologically (*ex-sistere*—to place outside) and as currently understood, this is so.

Since "being" means "to have a place in the realm of fact," this applies to "being" also.

Metaphysically "not-existing" and "not-being" are forms of "existing" and "being," and are therefore also objective.

It follows that the subject-counterpart of objects can only exist or be as an object, and that which is subjective can neither exist nor be at all.

II

To us? Of course, but *apart from us* there can be no question of being or existing. If there were, how could we know it? Everything we know depends upon us. Apart from us there is nothing that could be anything, for anything is only such because it is such to us. We cannot conceive of anything that is not conceived by ourselves.

Yet *we* could not conceive of anything if there were not something that had the faculty of conceiving. If the subject of objects is also an object, as has just been pointed out, there must be a further degree of subjectivity in order to account for the apparently subjective function of the object that is subject of all objects.[1]

III

Evidently it can neither be nor not be: it must transcend both, that is it cannot belong to a dimension known to us, for that which neither exists nor does not exist is not within the range of our faculties. It must be beyond our reach, unseizable, unknowable, inconceivable.

Yet, that which is neither being nor non-being, must also be that which we are, since everything we are and are able to know can only be due to that ultimate subjectivity which, nevertheless, to us inevitably is not.

Since *it is not*—we may not regard it as Pure Subjective Being, for that would be looking in the wrong direction, in the direction of that which is. Therefore we can only experi-ence this as ABSOLUTE ABSENCE.

But if existence (*ex-sistere*—to place or stand outside) in itself is *objective*, as has been stated, in-existence in its implied

---

[1] In case there should be a doubt about this: we who see objects as existing (place them outside) are ourselves seen as objects (placed outside).

sense of not-standing-outside-because-standing-within (*intra-sistere*),[2] must in itself be *subjective*—which is looking in the right direction, in the direction of that which is not. And that can only be experienced as ABSOLUTE PRESENCE.

IV

If we have understood this we have understood all the little that I know, and I can be of no further help.

The only service that even the Masters could render those who came to them was to turn them round, set them facing in the right direction, and place them with their backs to the object. They had nothing to teach, and they often said so.

But if the blindfold have anything to teach one another, it is this: go to the Awakened Masters—and leave all your baggage behind.

[2] That there is no English word, such as "intrasistence" for this tangential negative, which is really the absence of both existence and inexistence, that is their "vertical" transcendence, is quite normal, for the double negation required by metaphysical thinking has not hitherto been required by logical reasoning.

COLOPHON

Stepping into the public hall, His Reverence said,

"The knowledge of many things cannot be compared for excellence with giving up seeking for anything.

There are not different kinds of mind, and there is no doctrine which can be put into words.

As there is no more to be said, the assembly is dismissed!"

—HUANG PO, *Chün Chou Record*, 33

EPILOGUE

The transcendence of suffering-and-pleasure
Is attained not by wallowing in both
But by experiencing the inexistence of either

ABSOLUTE ABSENCE
is also
ABSOLUTE PRESENCE

But the absence of
PRESENCE-AND-ABSENCE
is the
INCONCEIVABLE TRUTH

Epilogue

93 ·- *Aspects of the Doctrine of Bodhidharma as Developed by the Patriarchs*

The void of annihilation is a single negative.

The void of Prajna is a double negative—the absence of an absence.

In the subjective dimension we are disidentified, detached: it is the voidness of voidness, the absence of presence-and-absence, that which neither is nor is not. Neither thinking nor not-thinking is the entrance to this state: it is beyond either and both—it is the absence of not-thinking.

The only sense in which we are one (single) is that in which we are all.

People seeking enlightenment via their own "egos," i.e. trying to lose their "selves" by means of themselves, are like somebody trying to forget himself by looking at himself in a mirror. In the old analogy they are precisely trying to pull themselves up by means of their own boot-straps.

Extension

All objects are in time and space. It is their extension in time and space that constitutes their unreality. Deprived of extension they would no longer be objects.

But that does not make them subjects: they have never been either subjects or objects in the "reality" of non-extension. They are the voidness of subjectivity.

The *bodhi*-mind is to be thought of as "vertical" because it is not subject to seriality or one-damn-thing-after-another, i.e. it has no extension in time—and extension of mind in space was never more than a conventional concept.

"Vertical" Mind and the Now-Moment

The Masters' insistence on the "purity" of the "Essence of Mind," on its imperviousness to pollution, is only explicable as an indication that Non-objectivity is *inaccessible* to phenomenal man. Phenomena, therefore, and also noumena, must be in a different *direction of measurement* from that of "Essence of Mind." This seems to be of particular importance for its realization, yet it has never been adequately stressed as far as I am aware.

"Birthlessness," permanence, eternality, as opposed to the transiency of phenomenal existence, indicate this direction of measurement, which has to be envisaged as being at right-angles to that of serial time. Its timelessness (which is the only eternity) is its essential nature for us. This means that the "vertical" mind could never be reached via the "horizontal" dimension, except at the point of intersection which is the now-moment.

The "Mysterious" Third Phase

In the third phase in which, having seen mountains and rivers as such and no longer as such, the awakened sees them once more as mountains and rivers, he no longer sees them as objects of himself as subject—for he knows that he is not that. There is, for him, just a see-ing in which there is no see-er or seen but just a suchness, an is-ness which is that-which-is, interpreted by the psycho-somatic mechanism as "mountains and rivers."

Epilogue

This is also an explanation of the third element in the Buddha's formula in the Diamond Sutra.

The Only Equality

All sentient creatures are necessarily equal as such, for their only "reality" is not as other sentient creatures' objects, but as pure subjectivity itself. Via each, in fact, the perceptible universe is created in objectivity, and there could be no hierarchy in the subjectivity which projects it. As other sentient creatures' objects they are as purely dreamed as the rest of the sensually perceived universe. The dreamed universe is interpretation subject to the seriality of time, in what I have termed the "horizontal" dimension.

Bubbles

A myriad bubbles were floating on the surface of a stream. "What are you?" I cried to them as they drifted by.

"I am a bubble, of course" nearly a myriad bubbles answered, and there was surprise and indignation in their voices as they passed.

But, here and there, a lonely bubble answered, "We are this stream," and there was neither surprise nor indignation in their voices, but just a quiet certitude.

94 ⁓ Man and Nature

Man always seems to have regarded Nature as his enemy and his prey, to be exploited and destroyed at will.

Even the Saints and Sages, with specific exceptions, seem at least tacitly to accept this arrogant absurdity; and those who include man among "sentient beings" sometimes appear to be unaware that plant-life also is sentient.

Objective man is an integral part of objective Nature, and could have no total superiority therein except in his own estimation. Subjective man merely is one with subjective Nature, for non-objectivity is undifferentiated and undifferentiable. The sensually interpreted universe is no more man's than it is beetle's.

In the degree in which he knows himself to be one with Nature, in just that degree is a man nearer to awakening. He is not required to "love" Nature instead of "hating" it: he is required to understand that he is it in so far as he is man.

95 ·- Inseeing

It is often said that see-er, see-ing, and seen, or experiencer, experiencing, and experiment, are one; this may, in a colloquial sense, be so. But it is also said that there is no see-ing without a see-er, no experience (experiencing or experiment) without an experiencer: this, however, is not so.

As far as I happen to know, only Krishnamurti seems to have expressed this correctly. Without a see-ing, an experiencing, there can be no see-er, no experiencer. Neither before nor after a see-ing, an experiencing, is there a see-er, an experience-er. The latter is produced in order to explain, or to justify, the phenomenon. In fact he has never existed, and never could exist: he is just a supposition invented *pour les besoins de la cause*—like the ether of an earlier generation of scientists, who thought that if it did not exist it jolly well ought to—in order to justify their ways of interpreting the sensually-perceived universe.

Epilogue

As so often pointed out heretofore, "see-ing," "experiencing," signify the cognition of all forms of manifestation, and indicate the "pure perception" which is subsequently interpreted as the apparent universe.

That which is "seen" or "experienced" is as imaginary as the "see-er" and "experience-er": both are interpretations of a movement in subjectivity which we term see-ing and experiencing.

96 – Vertical Living

The Kingdom of Heaven is the "vertical" mind.

The "vertical" mind is always present—in the Now-moment.

Intuition is an expression of the "verticality" of mind.

Non-attachment, non-abiding, non-conceptualising, non-daydreaming are all living "vertically" instead of "horizontally."

Metanoesis, *paravritti*, is turning over to the "verticality" of mind.

Self (in all forms of separateness) is "horizontal" living in serial time.

Ouspensky's "self-recognition," D.C. Harding's "headlessness," Shen Hui's "l'éveil simple," are "vertical" living.

All truth is "vertical": nothing "horizontal" can be true.

All true-*seeing* is "vertical."

All objects are "horizontal": subjectivity is "vertical."

The "vertical" is "real": the "horizontal" is "unreal."

In "vertical" living the I-fixation is no longer present.

Note: The term "vertical mind" is used as a convenience for "the verticality of Mind." Cf. "Vertical Vision," 1 and 2.

The terms "horizontal" and "vertical" are metaphorical and indicate that the one is in a different direction of measurement from the other. The one represents the objective direction, the other the subjective.

97 ᵔ "The Way of the Water"

Of all that has to be "laid down"—conditioning, knowledge, religion, science, "self," perhaps the most important is the idea that one lives his own life. To lay down the rest and go on thinking that one lives instead of being lived, would be an idle gesture. We do not "choose" to be born, to grow old, to be well or ill, or to die: why on Earth should we imagine that we can choose anything in between, i.e. how we live, let alone everything? We are free to understand, which means free to know ourselves as "vertical" mind—that is our one and only freedom, as I have often pointed out.

If "we" can "lay down" our fatuous and arrogant notion that we "live our own lives" instead of being lived integrally from birth to death, than "we" shall have laid down everything, not in detail but *en bloc*.

Freewill

"Horizontally" we have no freedom whatsoever—"vertically" there is neither freedom nor non-freedom. That is the answer.

Epilogue

98 ·~ The Illusion of Being

There can be no reality but that which we interpret as such sensorially. There can be no object, nor anything positive other than that which is so interpreted.

There can be no object without a subject, no positive without a negative; therefore beyond that dualism there cannot be either subject or object, positive or negative. Without a knower how could there be anything to be known as "reality"?

Looking for "reality" is some thing looked for by a subject, and some positive thing. And looking for "non-reality" is also some thing looked for by a subject, and some negative thing. Only that which is phenomenal can be "seen" by a "looker" or "known" by a "knower."

That is why, metaphysically speaking, searching for any thing, a positive thing termed "reality" or a negative thing termed "non-reality," is looking in the wrong direction.

When the Master of Mu-mon told him to look for the Great Bear in the Southern hemisphere he was telling his pupil to turn his back on the object in order to achieve understanding, that is awakening. But Mu-mon had to see that he must turn his back on the subject also. That really means understanding that the apparent subject is itself an object, that is a factor in the serial dimension of time. Therein everything is equally "real" and "non-real." That is why the formula so tirelessly repeated by the Masters was to reveal to us that the Truth is neither real nor non-real. They applied this formula to every imaginable "dharma," for it is applicable to every concept, and it is always, in perfect simplicity, just "neither is nor is not." Shen Hui and others describe it alternatively as "the absence of an absence."

It need not be difficult to see that neither positive nor negative can exist apart, and that positive and negative together produce a mutual cancellation of light and shade, that neither subject nor object can exist apart, and that subject and object together produce a mutual cancellation of knower and known. But that mutual cancellation whereby they become non-positive and non-negative, non-subject and non-object can never be the result of an act of "will": it is just that which obtains when the serial time-dimension of dualistic interpretation is inoperative in the now-moment.

The now-moment is the point of intersection at which the seriality of time is cut. But that which cuts it cannot be named without thereby making it an object of a subject—and therefore phenomenal. Herein lies the only difficulty in perfect understanding. Some Masters referred to it as *Prajna* which, translated as "Wisdom," is not even suggestive; Shen Hui referred to it as *Chih* which, translated as "Knowledge," is not even an indication. Han Shan told us that by "Prajna" the Buddha wished us to understand "Subject." That is indeed an indication, but it must not be taken as anything more precise, and all we need to remember is that it is not that subject which could ever in any circumstances be an object, that is that it is not any *thing* whatsoever. Let us think of it, if ever we must do that, just as Absolute Absence.

Since it could never be an object, it is idle to think of it as such, which means to think of it at all—for everything we think of thereby becomes an object. That surely is the reason why thinking is the barrier the Masters so constantly insist that it is. But we can remember that it is only absolute absence *to us* and that precisely when we insist on thinking about it , that is—it is only absolute absence *as phenomena*.

What, then, is it? That, evidently, can never be said—since it has no objective existence. Yet it must necessarily be what we are, all that we are—and there can be no "we" in it. It follows also that it must be all that anything is in any sense in which anything can be said to be at all.

Is it not just that which obtains in the direction of measurement at right-angles to that seriality of time which imposes dualistic interpretation upon us and so constitutes our phenomenal and only reality? Our serial dimension is a limitation, technically known as "ignorance," which produces the notion of individual subject and its objects, the negation of which, the recognition of which as a double absence, leaves us simply as what in fact we are. But until that recognition is established, the phenomena we appear to be temporally as subject, and to know as objects, are our only reality, and that which we intemporally are cannot appear otherwise than as inexistent. Since that cannot be cognised it must appear as void; since it is not in any sense objective or objectivisable it has to be referred to as emptiness.

Our conditioning that fosters positivity at the expense of negativity unbalances us and makes it difficult for us to envisage the double absence, the absolute absence of everything we cling to phenomenally. But that integral "laying down" of everything is the price we must pay, for it is ultimately our selves we must "lay down," if we would be free of limitation and integrate that which we are.

Note: The absolute absence of all phenomenality is at the same time the absolute presence of that which is.

99 ~ Time, and Time Again

As long as anyone tacitly accepts Time either as really existing, or even as the basis of consideration, he is only concerning himself with objectivity. Therein his interpretations may be correct phenomenally, but metaphysically or metaphenomenally they have no validity whatsoever, for outside phenomena there is no Time, and intemporally there can be no phenomena.

Time, in fact, is the crux of the matter, for all phenomena appear in the seriality of Time, and are directly dependent upon it.

In order to arrive at any kind of understanding of that which is not phenomenal the concept of Time must be discarded. The Truth is essentially neither objective nor temporal.

Even of an apparent intuition we must ask—"Is it subject to Time?"

Intemporality—absence of Time—is in fact that Absolute Absence which is that which is.

※

No thing either is in Time or is not in Time—for Time itself neither is nor is not.

The temporal is an expression of the intemporal, and Truth is the absence of the absence of temporality.

100 ~ Nothing but the Truth

Subject IS object: object IS subject. Each is an aspect of the other (or, they are aspects of one another).

As subject *and* object they are not (neither is): as subject-object, object-subject, they are—but, as such, that which they are is a suchness in the intemporal dimension (in intemporality).

Epilogue

That is why no thing, neither subject nor object, either is or is not, why any "thing" neither is nor is not, why the Truth, "that which is," is a double absence, the absence of an absence, or the absence of "is not" in Time, i.e. in the temporal dimension at right-angles to the intemporal dimension.

I do not know in what form of words this essential understanding could be more simply stated.

⚮

There is only a looking in the right direction, an orientation of mind. *Paravritti,* metanoesis, is, doubtless, just that. And no one does it, nor is anything done; it is pure doing.

101 ·— *The Nature of Phenomena*

It is the *seeing* of an object (form) that is in question: the object (form as an object) is illusory interpretation by split-mind, for it has no self-nature, and *an object is nothing but the seeing* (or other sensing) *of it.*

But all seeing is subjectivity functioning (Function of Principal).

Pure seeing, subjectivity functioning, therefore, is subjectivity looking at itself, which is why form is seen as void by the unenlightened who are looking in the correct direction.

No thing is then seen, which is called "void." Form and void are one form is void and void is form.

Objects (form) are phenomena produced by mind, and reflect mind. Properly seen, they represent, and so point to, their creator—that which they are (Principal whose Function caused them to appear).

So seen, that again is subjectivity (Function) looking at itself (Principal), and all that is seen is void. (An eye looking at itself could never see anything.)

Phenomena only appear to exist via and for sentient beings, whose appearance is phenomenal but who *are* as noumenon which, as Function of Principal, projects their appearance.

Note: The action of non-action is Function.

An object is the product of the functioning of subject.

The functioning of subject is always objectivising.

This is applicable to the Subject of subject-and-object which are its object.

Function is the act of every action, not that which is done.

102 ·– Principal and Function

The basic nature or Buddha-mind (the Dharmakaya) is the intemporal (noumenal) *subject*, which is subject of the (phenomenal) *object* which in divided-mind is represented by the subject-and-object of daily life.

That is to say that the intemporal Dharmakaya (basic nature, noumenon) projects in its functional aspect (which is one with its aspect as Principal), in every now-moment, the temporal (phenomenal) universe, as seen by us serially.

Noumenality, the noumenal "mind," is whole-mind which in the temporal (serial) direction of measurement necessarily splits and becomes dualist, functioning (for it is still Function) as subject-and-object.

That is the objective interpretation (interpretation from objectivity). Subjectively there is only the Absolute, *seen* (objectively) as Principal-and-Function, all of whose objectivisations are illusory, dreams, or self-reflections in an inter-preted time-sequence, none of which can be said to be.

Every thing knowable, therefore, neither is nor is not, as objectivisation, its sole existence being in its subjectivity (in subjective "mind") which is an ultimate impersonal undiffer-entiated I.

Every sentient being is that, subjectively as a sentient being, i.e. in all his sentiency, and objectively as an illusory phenomenon.

That means that all sentient beings in so far as they ARE (are intemporal) and subject are one (one in all and all in one), and in so far as they are objects (in time) they are mul-tiple.

That is why all sentient beings "have the Buddha-nature" and are intrinsically enlightened—for that alone is what they ARE.

Note: So much better expressed by the great sage: "The being of separate beings is non-separate being." (Chuang-tse, c. 369–c. 286 B.C.)

103 ·– A Tip for Teachers

Surely the persistent effort to make an object of subject is a perennial absurdity? If the Tao that can be named is not the eternal Tao, no presentation in the guise of an object can be the intemporal Subject.

Since the Truth that cannot be stated as object must there-fore necessarily be Subject, which cannot be presented in the guise of an object without ceasing to be what it is, why not for a change try presenting object in the guise of Subject, without which it cannot be anything at all?

By the way, did the Masters do anything else?

Note: All contemporary talking and writing is circumambulating the subject treated as an object. As such it constitutes a vicious circle. That is why the great Masters did not do it. That is why they just pointed. In pointing they used all six senses. Sight and hearing predominated in their technique, but action was the basis of their revelation. Why? Because the act of action is Function, which Itself is Its Principal.

104 ᐩ Gâteaux des Rois

"What is a talk that surpasses the teaching of the Buddha and Patriarchs?"
The Master replied, "Cake." (Yun Men)
"A cake is an inanimate thing which expounds the Dharma and reveals the self-natured Buddha." (Luk II, p. 194.)[1]

Note: Cakes are created by Mind and reveal Mind as their creator: "they (inanimate objects) are always expounding the Dharma vigorously without interruption." (Hui Chung of Nan Yang)

Void is phenomena viewed subjectively.
Phenomena are only the seeing thereof, and the objective seeing may be a cake. That, or any other, phenomenal object viewed subjectively, that is by looking at the seeing which creates its appearance, is void—because subjective "eye" is looking at itself, i.e. the seeing is turned on itself.
Objective seeing is phenomena.
Subjective seeing is void.

[1] *Ed. note: Chan and Zen Teaching, Vol. 2* by Charles Luk.

Form, therefore, (phenomena) is seen subjectively as void, and void is seen objectively as form (phenomena)

Form is always at the same time potential void: void is always at the same time potential form.

But that which is not-seen as void is Principal not-seen by Its Function, for Principal and Function are one.

105 ·- The "Abiding-Place"

The "non-abiding mind" is mind not abiding in time, for the concept of space cannot exist apart from the concept of time.

The time-verity, however, is the absence of the notions of time and of its antithesis, or, as we say, the absence of no-time (for time neither is nor is not).

Therefore not-abiding in time (the non-abiding mind) is an absence, the absence of (the notion of) no time.

But the absence of phenomenal time-and-no-time is a presence in intemporality. And not-abiding in time also represents an absence regarding phenomenal time.

Therefore the non-abiding mind (mind not abiding in time) indicates a presence (an abiding) in intemporality.

Note: The above is applicable also to space, and to space-time.

୧୬

Technically a "non-abiding mind" also implies mind which is not arrested by conceptualisation, mind assailed by percepts which nevertheless fall like rain on an impermeable surface, mind which reflects but does not absorb, mind which flows on like a river that no *object* can stop, mind that receives but does not interpret.

106 ·– Awakening

No objective process could lead to awakening, because awakening is from a dream, and a dream is a process of objectivisation, so that objectivising is going on dreaming.

Awakening, therefore, is bringing that process to a sudden end by ceasing to look in the wrong direction.

Box and Cox

Enlightenment is not the attainment of anything whatsoever: it is just the removal of a barrier, that of the concept of subject-I, which inevitably made it appear as enlightenment of *myself*—instead of that which is when I am not.

There is apparent I, and Not-I which is the very absence of me (the absence itself of me)—which *is* (is called) enlightenment, just as absence of "enlightenment" is precisely apparent presence of me. They are two sides of a coin—a dualism not a duality (two disparate objects).

A Bodhisattva does not seek to enlighten inexistent "others": inexistent as a self, that which he is destroys the illusion of the existence of "others" as such.

Satori Has No Objective Existence

No such thing as enlightenment, awakening, satori exists as an objective fact or event outside time. There is no occurrence in mind other than the eclipse of the I-notion which impeded see-ing. Therefore it cannot be studied or worked for. All such action would be like a surgical operation on an image.

Nothing happens to anything, nothing is changed, there is no psycho-somatic event at all; mind is unaffected. It is just the recovery of clear vision. It has no *objective existence:* it is a purely *subjective* adjustment.

It is not phenomenal: it has no direct body-mind impact.

It is entirely noumenal: its existence is intemporal, and it does not manifest phenomenally.

It is essentially impersonal—the *impersonalisation* of a pseudo-individual psyche.

It is a looking in the right direction: *it is a sudden understanding* that there is no I subject to time.

It is a displacement of the centre of gravity from temporality to intemporality, from the phenomenal to the noumenal. It is purely subjective.

Note: "There is nothing outside of the mind, nothing which can be worked on, and nothing to be enlightened." (Han Shan)

107 ⁓ The True and the False Negative

As long as we use positive terms we are blocking our own view: we cannot perceive the truth via the positive, because the positive is necessarily objective, which, no doubt, is why we like it, why we always turn to it instinctively, for that is how we are conditioned. Such terms are "Reality," "Awareness," "Mindfulness," and any number of others, all of which turn us in the wrong direction and lead us up to a blank wall.

However, in using the negative instead of the positive we are apt to fall into a verbal trap, a purely mechanical error that is due to the dualistic nature of language. The mere negative is nothing (Han Shan called it the void of annihilation), but true negative is not that at all. Photographically the negative of a positive is not nothing, but the exact counterpart of the positive. In fact the positive is the objective picture, whereas the negative is the reversal of light-and-shade from which the objective image derives; as such it represents subject.

Taking the terms referred to above, and reversing them from positive to negative, we have "unreality," "unawareness," "unmindfulness," all of which are just nothing. But that is not what we seek. So we may use the terms "Non-reality," "Non-awareness," "Mindlessness." But in using these terms do we know what we are trying to say—and, if so, do those who hear or read our words know what we mean? I fear not. I fear that this is one of the quicksands in which we sink when we pursue the path of metaphysics. Sometimes, especially in translating, we turn to the word "absence," but "absence of thought," of mind, of action, of form, does not really suggest the negative counterpart of the positive, but rather total absence of anything of the kind in question.

There is no doubt as to what the Masters meant. They said that Form *is* Void, and nothing but Void, and vice versa, that Samsara *is* Nirvana, and vice versa. Similarly Shen Hui makes it abundantly clear that *wu nien,* no-thought, is not absence of thought, total absence of all that is thought, which is nothing, the void of annihilation, but, on the contrary, that it is an exact counterpart, something that may appear "void" to us but is not so to the awakened. That something (the "very absence," the "absence itself") is the negative counterpart of the positive, its counterpart by accurate articulation, exactly the same in all respects save that what is light in the positive is shade in the negative, and vice versa.

We seem to know it in some connections. For instance people who have not realized the above differentiation will nevertheless perhaps state that out of Non-manifestation manifestation comes, thereby revealing that the negative is the subject of the positive. But explain it they do not; they leave it as a mystery, one of the many apparent mysteries in metaphysics. But there are no mysteries in metaphysics. There is only failure to understand the obvious. Non-manifestation is not the void of annihilation, nothingness, any more than it is some great mysterious entity. It is just the negative counterpart of positive manifestation. That which positively is any thing, negatively is not that any thing; and that which negatively is not any thing, positively is that thing; or that which positively is light negatively is shade, and that which negatively is shade positively is light. The Heart Sutra says it in as downright a manner as that of Moses in the Ten Commandments.

That is why Absence, by articulation between temporality and intemporality, become Presence—and vice versa.

How are we to extricate ourselves from this quagmire? One may ask, how can I know? Apart from profound under-standing applied to every case what can anybody do? There is no metaphysical language, only a jargon, and perhaps there never will be.

At least this much can be said: *we must avoid positive terms.* They are all concepts, all objects. "Reality," "Awareness," "Mindfulness," and all the many others, are road-blocks, barbed-wire entanglements, even moving avalanches or land-slides that will carry us down and bury us. "Negative Reality," "Negative Awareness," "Negative Mindfulness"? The capital letter so widely used *does not* turn the reader round in the right direction either: he remans in the world of positivity, looking at, or for, something. The apposition of negative to positive, photographically, produces a blank; does it not do the same here? You look for a negative-positive: is that not a blank (which is still a positive)? I fear we can only use the negative—not the negative of annihilation with "un" or "in," but the negative with "non," remembering that it is not a total absence that is being pointed at (for it cannot be seen), but a total presence (that cannot be seen either), a total presence that is never any thing, seen by a see-er, known by a know-er, but just a pure see-ing or know-ing that is nowhere without.

Note: It may not be clear to everybody what is meant by "articulation." You have seen a skylight that is manipulated by two rods hinged to a cross-piece fixed to the wall? When you pull *down* the handle—the skylight goes *up* by articulation, and when you push *up* the handle—the skylight comes *down* again. Our muscular system works in the same manner; every contraction produces, by articulation, a decontraction in the complementary muscle, and the contraction of that muscle produces a decontraction in the first.

108 ·— Still Life

Function implies the concept of Movement,
    Movement implies the concept of Direction (dimensions for the measurement of movement),
    Direction implies the concept of Space (in which movement can occur),
    Movement in Space implies the concept of Time (in order to measure such movement).

Working back through the fundamental concepts which are the framework of our phenomenal universe, we arrive at Function—which is Principal manifesting by apparent Movement in apparent Space measured in three apparent Directions spatially and in one apparent Direction temporally (future to past via a theoretical present).

All apparent things are events occurring subject to these concepts, such events being movements of mind within this framework and taking place according to an apparent but illusory process of cause and effect.

❦

When Time stops phenomena disappear.

Phenomena are in function of Time.

Events depend upon seriality: they represent a dimension of the time-concept.

Phenomena are spatial concepts subject to Time, and Space itself is one such concept.

Events seem to be phenomenal effects of causes operating in the time-sequence.

Events, dependent on seriality, may constitute a second dimension of the time-concept.

109 ·~ Subjective Awareness

Subject and object can never be one in "things," i.e. as objects, but they are one in their objective extinction in Subjectivity.

I have previously pointed out that the subject of objects is only apparently such, and accordingly I have called it pseudo-subject, for both subject and object are themselves objects of pure subjectivity. It has also been stated that no object is or exists, and Huang Po, who tells us that by a perception that subject and object are one we shall awaken, also tells us to beware of clinging to one half of a pair.

The vital factor is that temporally there is a *solution de continuité* between subject and object—an absolute break, for concepts are consecutive in time. The only connection between them is via pure subjective awareness which is outside the seriality of time. That is why they are not as either, and why they cannot be as both. Neither is, both are not. Their dual negation leaves them as that which they are, as that which from the awakened state, projects them as a dualism, subject to time and henceforth apart forever. Their dependence is upon that which projects them, and their apparent interdependence is in function of that also.

The futility of attempting to unite them in thought should now be evident: they are united not in their existence but in their mutual inexistence.

Articulation, 1

As with *wu nien,* absence of thought and of no-thought, *wu hsin,* absence of mind and of no-mind, *wu sheng,* absence of existing and of non-existing, *wu wei,* absence of doing and of not-doing, all are discrete projects separate in time (as are any two thoughts), whose absolute absence phenomenally is an absolute presence intemporally. Their negation does not plunge them into the void of annihilation: by a process of articulation it transforms them precisely into THIS which intemporally is. That is the identity of "Form" and "Prajna-Void," of "Samsara" and "Nirvana," and the answer to such questions as arise in the Diamond and Heart Sutras.

Articulation, 2

This which things are is also perceived as the apparent functioning, in time, of Principal, which is immutable. This functioning involves three "aspects" of consciousness—(1) pure subjective awareness, which IS, (2) the seeing aspect—which we interpret as see-er or subject, and (3) that which is seen—or sense-data which are interpreted as objects.

Epilogue

This explains the Masters' manner of teaching which always avoided objective exposition: they demonstrated Function, never described it, they pointed, rarely revealed. The former is "looking" in the right direction, the latter in the wrong. Perception of that which is Function-*ing* via the Masters elicits a response which may be recognised as that which is Function-*ing* via the disciple in his response. "*That* which is . . ." is "*This* which is . . . ," one and the same. If the disciple recognised this, and returned with it to immutable Principal whose functioning in temporality it represents, he found himself to be this, *herein*—and awake.

That, no doubt, is the true manner, as practised by Bodhidharma, the Patriarchs and the T'ang Masters. But we have them not. What can we do but seek to understand? When the pseudo-mystery is dissolved we have to find a means of transforming that necessarily objective understanding, which, let us remember, is in itself nothing whatsoever, i.e. a total absence, by articulation into its counterpart—the total presence of THIS which is.

☙

The state of Awareness
Is
I-less I am.

Wu Nien

"Action kills thought," you say?
Yes, indeed, the kind of thought that is better dead.

"What, then, is the better kind of thought?"
Action itself is the better kind of thought.

110 ·- This

The objective universe, called *Samsara,* is a subjective illusion, and *positive.*

Its negative counterpart, which is also a subjective illusion, is called *Nirvana.*

Both are subject to the concept of Time, and are therefore phenomenal.

Beyond, or "at right-angles-to," the conceptual framework of Movement in Space measured by Time (Space-Time in motion), that is in Intemporality, there can only be pure subjective consciousness, which must be voidness to us, since it is an eye looking at itself.

THIS cannot be named without thereby becoming an object, which it can never be, and for the same reason THIS cannot be thought of.

All we can say of it is that THIS must be the such-ness, is-ness, quiddity of all of us sentient beings who, singularly and collectively, are its objective manifestation, and subjectively are its own functioning.

111 ·- This Which Is...

We are being lived? Nonsense: there is no such "we": "we" are not objects.

It is *we* who do the living of the puppet mistaken for us. But this "we" is pure subjective mind.

It is the apparent Functioning of Absoluteness (Isness) which is causing things to be seen via the appearance that bears our name.

This Latency apparently Functioning via the sentiency of sentient beings is known as *Prajna,* but the apparent action is a temporal illusion, for there is no actor outside time, but a latent function*ing* only.

This functioning of latency is the only You, ultimately never a "you," or ten thousand "yous," but the only "I."

∝

"Ask a wooden puppet
When it will attain Buddhahood
By self-cultivation."

—Yung-Ch'ia

112 ·- The Meaning of Pure Mind

The Masters' insistence on the purity of mind, that in itself it is intrinsically pure, and that its reflex in temporality must be purified—often in the metaphor of the removal of dust from a mirror, is apt to puzzle those to whom "purity" connotes something ethical. They come to realize that there is nothing particularly moral about this "purity," so they assume that what is meant is "chemical" purity—that is absence of any admixture with a substance other than itself.

That is still not quite the true meaning, and it would not account for so much insistence on the "unsullied" state of pure Mind. What is meant is that pure Mind is exclusively non-objective, utterly unsullied by the presence of any object. Similarly the cleansing of the reflex mind that operates in the seriality of time means its ridding of conceptualization. The dust that has to be removed from the surface of the mirror is the dust of objectivisation. All objects are to be wiped off it— so that it may be in correct relation with pure Mind, for without that correct relation Awakening cannot occur or obtain. But such relation can only be established between This-which-we-are and a reflex mind that, although subject to the seriality of time, is, at least momentarily, objectively "pure."

Pure Mind is integrally subjective in the sense that it is totally devoid of objectivity. That is why it is objectively void—for anything that is not "void" is an object, and voidness means absence of objects. It is void because it is our chemically-pure subjectivity looking at itself, and, whatever an eye may be as an object, it cannot see itself as a subject.

The importance of this is indicated by the Masters' continual insistence upon it. So-doing they are pointing at that which they seek to avoid saying directly—for, above all, they want their disciples to come to their understanding from within and not from without. Surely they were right, but we have them not—and we must be told.

113 ⌐ A Clean Sweep

Turn the river Alpheus through the Augean stables of your mind, and let it sweep away all objectivity therein.

Or ransack that temporal mind, collect every object that you can find therein, build a bonfire of them, place your self on the top of it—and light it. Then you may find that you are free—and awake.

But instead of being the subject of all that trash, you will be the Subjectivity of the entire universe. Not, of course, in the sense of a monarch knowing himself as such, but rather as the Latency of all Appearance, the Potentiality of all Actuality, or Primordial Consciousness.

Epilogue

114 - According to the Supreme Vehicle

Pure Apperceiving is the subjective Functioning of
Potential,
Sense-perception is its temporal reflex in objectivity,
Phenomena are a conceptual interpretation of that.

Therefore
That which they are
Is the mind that is perceiving them.

True Apperceiving is perceiving that, as mind, you are
bringing into apparent existence whatever you perceive.

Consequently
The fundamental nature of all phenomena
Is the Apperceiving of it.

According to Vedanta

This has been expressed colloquially in the words:

That which is manifested in taking Name and Form
Emerges from That-Which-Is-Mobile (Function).
That-Which-Is-Mobile
Emerges from That-Which-Is-Immobile (Immutable
Principal).
Awakening is the relation established between Pure
Existence
And that which resembles It in whoever has the experience.
(subjective Functioning of Potential and senseperception)

Note: All words denote an object, for language is a dualistic medium, but a few words—such as "this," "here," "now"—point in the right direction, whereas others—such as "that," "there," and "then"—point away from this which we are. Vedanta ignores this technicality, but we have no Gurus but the printed word and may be well-advised to neglect nothing that may help to turn us away from the positive and the objective, which are for us a *route sans issue.*

According to Sufism

"Thou seest nought in the world but Me" does not just mean, in its general sense, that everything you can perceive is "God," true as that may seem to be—for that is perfectly dualistic (requiring see-er and seen, man and God).

It seeks to indicate that everything thou seest thou, as godhead, createst in the seeing of it. I create every object via the perceiving of it, as you do—for you and I are one as godhead—no matter what may be perceived nor by whatever sentient being, who *in* perceiving always is godhead, for the perceiving, no matter what is perceived, is all that sentient being Is.

Neither the sentient being nor "God" exists as an object, but the subjective Function in its functioning only.

That is: "There is nought in the world but *this which I am* or this which you are, for all that WE ARE is godhead."

∝

"Busy thyself with Me, not thee," does not just mean, in its general sense, that you should concern yourself with "God" and not with your self, true as that may seem to be—for that too is perfectly dualistic.

It seeks to indicate that it is only as godhead that you ARE, and that as an object—"thee"—you are not.

That is "Recognise thyself as *this which thou art.*"

❧

"When the Infinite doth appear, thereat thou vanishest,
For 'thou' hast never been, from first until last.

Thou seest not who thou art, for thou art, yet art not 'thou'."

That is: "Thou art the Infinite and nothing else—for there is no object called 'thou.'"

❧

"I then am Absolute in Essence, Infinite,
My only 'where' is 'through Myself I am.'"

"Since there is no room in the Infinite even for nothing ness, I cannot be nothing; and since the Infinite has no parts, I am therefore the Whole." (Note by Martin Lings in *A Moslem Saint*, p. 202; quotations from Shaikh Ahmad Al Alawi [1870–1932] ibid., pp. 200, 210.)

Even "nothingness" is an object, and "I" cannot be that. *This which is,* whatever phenomenal appearance it may have as an object in Time, must be the one whole that is infinite.

This is the pure doctrine in Muslim terms, nearer Vedanta than Ch'an.

❧

"Extinction also is one of thine attributes. Thou art already extinct, my brother, before thou art extinguished and naught before thou art annihilated.

"Thou art an illusion in an illusion and a nothingness in a nothingness. When hadst thou Existence that thou mightest be extinguished?

"Thou art *as a mirage in the desert that the thirsty man taketh to be water until he cometh unto it and findeth it to be nothing, and where he thought it to be, there findeth he God.*"

When the thirsty man reached the apparent water, that is the mirage called "thou," all he found was Godhead. But he did not "find" even that: he brought it—he himself *was* it. (Shaikh of our Shaikhs Mawlay Al Arabi ad Darqawa [c. 1809] op. cit., p. 137.)

Note: It may be asked, "Why not also 'ACCORDING TO CHRISTIANITY'?" Are we not conditioned to Christianity? Must we "burn the Gospels in order to read Hui Neng," as Dr. Benoit asked? No, it was the Christian Churches that did the burning in order to impose their exoteric doctrine. We need only read Dionysius. Eckhart, van Ruysbroeck, St. John of the Cross—to name a few that are readily accessible—in order to find the same teaching, in so far as that could be expressed without incineration, and in slightly different terminology. It is possible also to re-read the words of Jesus Himself with insight instead of outsight. Christianity is our own personal affair.

NOTE ON THE DIAMOND SUTRA

I would like to remind anyone reading this of the words of Hui Neng, the Sixth Patriarch, in the *T'an Ching* or Platform Sutra itself. Having announced his approaching death, his disciples were moved to tears, with the exception of Shen Hui (here called Shin Wui in Southern Chinese, as Hui Neng is called Wei Lang):

"Young Master Shin Wui (then aged 45) is the only one here who has attained the state of mind which sees no difference in good or evil, knows neither sorrow nor happiness, and is unmoved by praise or blame."

After this significant pronouncement he castigates the others for the ignorance betrayed by their sentiment, proving that they had not understood. Shen Hui was thereby revealed as the successor and guardian of the pure doctrine. (Wei Lang, p. 114.)

Shen Hui, an enlightened sage, whom Dr. Suzuki calls "the most eloquent disciple of Hui Neng" (No-Mind, p. 29) justifies these our expectations of him, and is one of the select company who can really help us, and on whom we can rely. Here we have an example.

In reply to a question regarding the gatha in the Diamond Sutra whose efficacy is extolled with such hyperbole, he agrees that the gatha in question here is that which contains the words:[1]

---

[1] There are four in this category in the Diamond Sutra: the one he selects is Sect. 23, p. 61, in Conze. Mr. Price seems to leave this passage partially untranslated.

"Absence of the phenomena of self, other, beings and age."[2]

But he points out that it is only because there are these phenomena that one speaks of their absence. The sense, he says, is not that given these lines by the masters (maîtres de la loi), for it is the absence itself of this absence of phenomena that is the real meaning of the "gatha of four lines," and which renders it of such inestimable value as a means to enlightenment.[3]

This should now be obvious. Shen Hui restores or represents these lines as the Buddha's essential formula: (a) the phenomena exist as such; (b) on that account they (also) are not (are "absent")—*wu*—which is the Prajnaparamita doctrine applicable to all phenomena; (c) therefore they are. But here he actually tells us what this final phase is—and it is a negative, the absence (*wu*) of the absence of phenomena (the "very absence" which is itself a presence).[4]

[2] These are the same four terms that are given as near synonyms in most of the English versions—ego-entity, personality, being and separated individuality (Price), or self, being, soul, person (Conze). The French sinologist's version evidently has greater verisimilitude as regards "self" and "other," though "age" may appear slightly inapposite. The sense might have been "time" or "beings in time." "Life" is the sense currently given in China today.

[3] The "absence itself" of an absence is a presence, a point emphasised by Shen Hui also in connection with wu-nien, where he treats of the absence of thought as the essential presence. This negatively implied presence is Truth itself which, not being objective or objectivisable, cannot be stated in positive terms which would thereby render it that which it can never be.

[4] It may be necessary to insist on the fundamental identity of all interdependent counterparts. This is fully explained elsewhere, but, in brief: absence is negative, presence is positive, so that their mutual negation, in the reunion of the counterparts, unites non-positive with non-negative, which is absence of both, a total absence or void. The absence, like the void, is phenomenal.

Note on the Diamond Sutra

We can now see that the Buddha's formula is really the resolution of all so-called dualities—which is the mutual negation of both elements, i.e. the void or voidness.

Henceforth we may say that the form of words in which the third phase of the Buddha's formula is rendered no longer greatly matters[5]—for what it implies is now luminously clear. It is the epitome of the doctrine of the Prajnaparamita itself. All that remains is to realize the resplendent negativity of very voidness.[6] (See *Entretiens du Maître de Dhyana Chenhouei du Ho-tsö*, Hanoi 1949, p. 47. Jaques Gernet. Publications de l'Ecole Française d'Extrème Orient.)

[5] The fairly current translation "is called" such and such, meaningless in itself and apparently a repetition of the first phase of the formula, can now be interpreted in the sense that "it is called" because it is not in fact such, i.e. it is the negative, or absence, of the previous phases of the formula, which are purely conceptual.

[6] Let us not forget that the void, or voidness, also is purely conceptual. Shen Hui himself remarks; "The void no longer exists for those who have seen, (their) self-nature." The translation "seen" is inacceptable, for self-nature cannot be seen dualistically, and this makes nonsense of the profound truth that is here being revealed. No doubt the pictogram can mean "to see," but in this context it evidently indicated something such as "recognised (themselves as)" or "apperceived self-nature." Huang Po says: Why this talk of seeing into your own nature?" "That Nature and your perception of it are one" (p. 116). Voidness is a means of indicating that which, being beyond the apprehension of the dualistic process of thinking, appears as vacuity. The words "their self-"represent an unfortunate initiative on the part of translators, the Chinese term being "nature" only. The "self" is that of "nature," if implied, not of any individual. "Their (fundamental) nature" or "nature itself" give the true sense. (Citation. op. cit., p. 43.)

General Note: It may be remembered that in Sect. 5, p. 28, Conze, the translation of one of the Buddha's statements of his formula doubles the negative: "What has been taught by the Tathagata as the possession of marks, that is truly a no-possession of no marks." Since the Buddha's formula is applied to every imaginable category of dharma we can re-express this example as follows: "What has been taught as the presence of phenomena is truly the absence of no-phenomena." That is precisely the formula, cited above, stated by Shen Hui to be the true sense. It is not possible for me to know how it comes to appear here only, and only from Dr. Conze even here, but he is far too exact a scholar to have made a mistake of that kind in inserting it. One may be inclined to wonder whether in faulty texts the true rendering may not have been preserved by accident in this case. Copyists who think they understand a text whose real meaning is quite beyond their comprehension are capable of just such an enormity.

The "possession" of marks must be understood to mean such "reality" or verity as there may be in the idea of the possession of marks. Thus it could be said that: "What has been taught by the Tathagata as (the presence of) Samsara (that which Samsara is or can be said to be) is truly the absence of non-Samsara." The Truth is neither Samsara nor non-Samsara. That does not merely depend on the negative aspect of Samsara, but on the mutual negation of both Samsara and its opposite as concepts. The word translated "possession" (*sampad*) also means "excellence" and "attainments," i.e. that which "they become," thus indicating that which the "marks" really represent. (See Conze, p. 28.)

This is so important that it may be worth further exegesis. "The absence of no-phenomena" here does not imply the presence of the negative counterpart of "phenomena," that is

Note on the Diamond Sutra

"one half of a pair" and the "void of annihilation" of Han Shan; it is not just non-Samsara. It is the *Non-Manifestation from which manifestation arises,* the "Voidness of Prajna," the "Void of Absoluteness," as Han Shan calls it, or pure Potential (*ta chi*). This is precisely the point that Han Shan makes, and which he declares that the Buddha sought to make us understand. (See Han Shan's Commentary on the Diamond Sutra, tr. by Charles Luk in *Ch'an and Zen Teaching,* 1st Series.) The contrary is the error of the "Maîtres de la Loi" of which Shen Hui speaks, and which he avoids by using the double absence or negative, which accords with the formula of the Masters— "neither is nor is not"—the Truth being expressible only by indicating the absence of both phenomenal counterparts—phenomena and non-phenomena.

It should be realized that this is no minor technical point of doctrine, but the very absence of doctrine which reveals the direct path.

Analysis

Let us take the simplest case—"sym-pathy" and "anti-pathy," which are contradictory interpretations of "*pathein*" (to feel). The absence of both interpretations, i.e. neither feeling-with nor feeling-against, leaves you with pure perceiving uninterpreted. "Suffering and pleasure (anti-suffering)" are identical with the above, as are "love and hate." None of these interpretations either are or are not, exist or do not exist veritably, for their verity lies only in the uninterpreted perceiving, i.e. they are not as interpretations, but they are not basically inexistent on account of the perceiving (apparent Functioning of the Absolute) underlying the interpretation, which itself, uninterpreted, is not in the serial dimension of time.

193

Every phenomenon, thing, concept, object, neither is nor is not. As an interpretation it is not, but it is not inexistent (its absence connotes a presence) as that which it is not (as its absence), for that, uninterpreted, is pure perceiving (Functioning), not on the part of a subject in time, but intemporally.

In the serial time-dimension of phenomenal experience many apparent opposites and complementaries can find composition. For instance treble-and-base, hot-and-cold, long-and-short have a mediate term, which is neither. Suffering-and-pleasure also can have a mediate term which is neither, and which can be called non-suffering and non-pleasure (they are the "void of annihilation" of Han Shan). But these are entirely conceptual and objective and have no metaphysical significance. Metaphysical significance lies exclusively in their double absence, and can only be indicated by that. Their foundation in the non-serial, intemporal direction of measurement, which is "void" to us perceiving as subjects of objects, can only be indicated by directing attention towards the absence of their existence as that which is interpreted as well as the absence of the negation of that, i.e. the absence of hot-and-of-not-hot, of cold-and-of-not-cold, of each member of each pair of opposites or complementaries and of its negation or opposite. Attention so directed is turned away from the serial dimension of subject-and-object, which are thereby reunited in transcendence, and is thus rendered available for reintegration in intemporality.

That should be the reason of the efficacy of the Buddha's formula, its patent success in the persons of Subhuti and Hui Neng, in that of Wu Men and so many others, and of the paeons of hyperbolic praise, which it receives in the Diamond Sutra itself.

Note on the Diamond Sutra

Apperceiving double absence, "the absence itself of absence," i.e. perceiving an absence itself as a presence, is non-objective vision—which is the only Truth.

Note on "Wu-nien"

The concept "not-thinking" is an object of subject as is its counterpart the concept "thinking."

That is why the Masters stated that sitting with a blank mind or forcibly suppressing thoughts are not the path to true seeing (in-seeing).

Therefore the presence (in intemporality) represented in time by the absence of thought (*wu-nien*) is not the concept, or psychic action, of "not-thinking," but that which intemporally corresponds to the formula "thought *neither* is *nor* is not," the double absence of Thought and of No-thought, which is pure Functioning (*ta yung*).

That is the in-seeing of true nature to which the Masters pointed: phenomenally an absolute absence, intemporally an absolute presence.

If anyone desires more familiar authority than I have cited he has only to turn to our old friend and good teacher, the enlightened monk Hui Hai (tr. John Blofeld, 1948), pp. 34 and 35, on each of which pages he expounds with commendable lucidity the essence of what I have sought to explain herein. He ends the second description with this phrase:

"If this principle is understood, that will amount to real deliverance, *for the attainment of which there can be no other method.*"

LET ME REMIND YOU

"Let me remind you
That the perceived
Cannot perceive."

—HUANG PO

If you should ever come to understand the full significance of this, will you not have understood everything that needs to be understood?

$\mathcal{INDEX}$

See also Table of Contents
References are to the numbered sections

Index

Doctrine of, 14; Flower Sermon, 52; Formula of, 27, 33, 66, 77; Naughty, 22; Regarding Nirvana, 41; Meaning of Prajna, 98; Transmission of doctrine, 10; Ultimate teaching of, 60
Buddhism, 39, 73

Cabbages-of-the-garden, 58
Cake, 37, 104
Caritas, 12, 38
Causation, 23
Cause (and Effect), 88
Cause: Immediate and ultimate, 88
Ch'an: Introduction, 10, 17, 21, 34, 63, 114
Chang Chen Chi, 69
Charity, 35
Chuang-tse, 1; Part II (title page), 102
Chiao: Doctrine, 77
Chih: Introduction, 66, 98
Chin, Master, 77
China, 73
Christianity, 10, 17, 114
Christians, 39
Chunder Bose, 37
Clown, 4
Consciousness: Conditioned aspect of, 74; the Eight, 77; no Entity, 8; Growth of a second, 36; Pure, 12, 14, 18, 40, 43, 60; in Sat-Chit-Ananda, 68; as Subjectivity, 75; as Vertical vision, 79; as Void of Subjectivity, 68
Compassion, 36, 37, 38

Conze, Dr. Edward, 24, 27, *D. Sutra*
Counterparts, 66; Interdependant, *D. Sutra;* Uniting of, 79

Death, 8
Delusion, 52
Desire, 13
Dharma, 27, 60, 104
Dharmas 23, 24, 27, 63
Dbarmakaya, 102
Dbyana, Intro., 69, 90
Dimensions, 18
Dionysius, 114
Direction, 108
Discrimination, 30
Distillation, 38
Dogmas, 39
Dogs, 38
Donkeys, 39, 58
Dream(s): Awakened from, 87; Definition, 67; the Dreamed as objects, 93; the Living Dream, 42; Mumon on, 54; Sleeping, 38, 60; *Sosie* 40; Two degrees of, 38; the Waking-, 16, 60
Duality, 64, 86; Non-, 66, 70
Dualities, 65 (note)
Dualism, 10, 20, 21

Eckhart, 114
Ego. *See* I-concept
Egoism, 13
Emptiness. *See* Void
E-myo, 53
Enlightenment, 27, 30, 38, 85, 106; By Hearing, 77 (note)

Index

Index

Index

Moses, 107
Mosquito, 37
Mountains and Rivers, 60, 77, 84, 93
Movement, 73, 108
Mu-mon, 53, 54, 55, 77, 98
Muslim, 39, 114

Nakedness, 1, 47
Name and Form, 114
Nature, 24, 34
Negation, of Void, 66
Negative: Double, 93; and Positive, 32; -Way, 38, 62
Neti Neti, 66 (note)
Nirvana, 3, 22, 23, 41, 42, 47, 48, 60, 65, 77
Nirvanically, 48
No-doctrine, Col.
No-entity, 5, 18
No-thought, 107
No thingness, 80
Non-action, 8
Northern Sect, 90
Noumenon, 24, 41, 46, 88
Now-moment, 21, 93
Nyanatiloka Thera, 83

Oak tree in the Garden, 55
Object, 8; Spatial, 81
Objectivity, 52
Ocean, 49
Opposites, 18, 78
Origen, 39

Paramita, 67
Paravritti, 63, 77, 96, 100
Past, 8
Path, 8, 100

Pathien, D. Sutra
Patriarch, Fifth, 62
Patriarchs, 109
Perceiving, 87
Perception, 27; Pure, 50, 51, 84 (note)
Persona (mask), 47
Phenomena, 3, 11, 18, 41
Photograph, 33, 65, 66, 107
Plants, 37
Plenum, 20, 24, 27
Positive (and Negative), 24, 33, 60, 66
Potential, *D. Sutra*
Prajna, Intro., 12, 90; Wisdom, 56, 98, 111
Presence (and Absence), 20, 42, 89
Presence, Universal, 11
Present, The, 3, 8, 14
Price, A.F., 27, *D. Sutra*
Pride, 8, 13, 36
Psychologists, 86 (note)

Quiddity, 110

Radiation, 36
Ramakrishna, 39, 47
Real, 18
Reality: As Being, 24; As Concept, 61; As Consciousness, 18; Dimensional Interpretation, 35; Inexistence of, 68; Intemporal, 15, 38; Negative, 28; As Non-Reality, 27; Perception of, 33; As Phenomenon, 25; As Positive, 107; Purely Objective, 91, 98; Relative-, 33, 42, 46; Not Relative, 42; as Void, 40

Index

Index

Sentient Publications, LLC publishes books on cultural creativity, experimental education, transformative spirituality, holistic health, new science, and ecology, approached from an integral viewpoint. Our authors are intensely interested in exploring the nature of life from fresh perspectives, addressing life's great questions, and fostering the full expression of the human potential. Sentient Publication's books arise from the spirit of inquiry and the richness of the inherent dialogue between writer and reader.

We are very interested in hearing from our readers. To direct suggestions or comments to us, or to be added to our mailing list, please contact:

SENTIENT PUBLICATIONS, LLC

1113 Spruce Street
Boulder, CO 80302
303.443.2188
contact@sentientpublications.com
www.sentientpublications.com